Exploring the Field of Business Model Innovation

Oliver Gassmann • Karolin Frankenberger • Roman Sauer

Exploring the Field of Business Model Innovation

New Theoretical Perspectives

palgrave
macmillan

Oliver Gassmann
Institute of Technology Management
University of St. Gallen
St. Gallen, Switzerland

Karolin Frankenberger
Strategic Management and
Entrepreneurship
University of Lucerne
Lucerne, Switzerland

Roman Sauer
Institute of Technology Management
University of St. Gallen
St. Gallen, Switzerland

ISBN 978-3-319-41143-9   ISBN 978-3-319-41144-6   (eBook)
DOI 10.1007/978-3-319-41144-6

Library of Congress Control Number: 2016953646

Cover illustration Mono Circles © John Rawsterne/patternhead.com

Printed on acid-free paper

This Palgrave Macmillan imprint is published by Springer Nature
The registered company is Springer International Publishing AG Switzerland

PRAISE FOR *EXPLORING THE FIELD OF BUSINESS MODEL INNOVATION*

"Professors Gassmann, Frankenberger and Sauer pack a great deal of important research into a surprisingly readable and compact format. This volume will be essential reading for academics working on the study of business model innovation. It will also be quite helpful for people in industry who seek a broader perspective as they search for ways to enhance an existing business model, or to disrupt an incumbent's business model."

Prof. Henry Chesbrough,
UC Berkeley

"This book fills a much needed gap: with great clarity Gassmann and Frankenberger explain that there are 7 ways that managers, students and researchers can utilize business models to think more clearly about business problems – and they provide a vivid illustration to make this come alive."

Prof. Charles Baden-Fuller,
Cass Business School, London

"This book provides a comprehensive, perhaps even exhaustive, guide to the state of the art of business model research. If you want to get to grips with this important issue, Professor Gassmann's new book tells you everything you need to know."

Prof. Julian Birkinshaw,
London Business School

"This book is an outstanding and comprehensive piece of work regarding different schools of thought in business development and linking them with major theories. Where articles normally lack in the big picture, this books provides an astonishing easy way to understand current and future research in business modeling and help to find your own position."

Prof. Ellen Enkel,
Chief Editor of R&D Management

"Without a doubt, the most comprehensive and well-researched survey of the literature on business models and business model innovation. A must read for anyone aiming to understand the origins, current state, and future prospects of this important and growing field of management research."

Prof. Ramon Casadesus-Masanell,
Harvard Business School

"A comprehensive overview of the current state-of-the-art of the business model literature, and a useful primer on possible theoretical perspectives that could help push the boundaries of the field. Short and punchy – a great Business Model *Theory* Navigator!"

Prof. Christoph Zott,
IESE Business School

ACKNOWLEDGEMENTS

We would like to thank Jae-Yong Lee, Daniel Straimer, and Alissa Siara for supporting us in the editing and for their research assistance. Our thanks also go to Ellen Enkel who provided valuable thoughts on improvement and Liz Barlow and Maddie Holder from Palgrave Macmillan for the good cooperation.

Contents

LIST OF FIGURES

LIST OF TABLES

AUTHOR BIOGRAPHIES

Oliver Gassmann is a full professor at the University of St. Gallen, Switzerland, where he is also Director of the Institute of Technology Management. Gassmann has published several books and more than 350 articles in leading journals. In 2014, he was honoured as one of the world's leading innovation scholars by IAMOT and has been awarded with the Scholary Impact Award by Journal of Management.

Karolin Frankenberger is Assistant Professor for Strategic Management and Entrepreneurship at the University of Lucerne, Switzerland, and founder of the BMI lab. Frankenberger previously worked for several years as a consultant at McKinsey & Company, and her research has been published in leading journals such as Academy of Management Journal or R&D Management.

Roman Sauer is a research associate at the Institute of Technology Management, University of St. Gallen, Switzerland, and also works as a consultant for the BMI lab. He received a diploma in mechanical engineering from the Technical University Munich, Germany.

CHAPTER 1

Introduction

Abstract Business models have received significant attention from both practitioners and academics. Research has been accelerated within the last decade to understand the phenomenon better. This chapter introduces the reader to the vibrant research field and its increasing relevance. It explores common themes and concepts in the field by presenting a broad overview. Business model research is still heterogeneous, and progress is made only incrementally at the moment. Hence, this section discusses the need to organize the field better and to thoroughly interlink the concept with theoretical perspectives as this could improve the generalizability of business model studies.

Keywords Business models • Business model innovation • Relevance of the field • State of the literature

Business model innovators, such as Amazon, Skype, and Uber have revolutionized their industries by overcoming the dominant industry logic. Amazon became the biggest bookseller in the world without owning a single brick-and-mortar store; Skype is the largest telecommunications provider worldwide without having any network infrastructure at its disposal; Uber revolutionized the taxi business and reached to a market capitalization of more than 50 billion dollars within a few years

© The Editor(s) (if applicable) and the Author(s) 2016
O. Gassmann et al., *Exploring the Field of Business Model Innovation*,
DOI 10.1007/978-3-319-41144-6_1

without employing a single taxi driver and without owning any taxi cars. However, *Business Model Innovation* (BMI) is not only restricted to the innovative Silicon Valley companies. By contrast, it has become an important management issue for all companies under margin and competitive pressures. Companies like BASF, Bosch, IBM, PepsiCo, Sennheiser, Siemens, and Toshiba are actively developing new business models for building up sustainable competitive advantages. Whole industries like the energy and health sector are undergoing a radical transformation, and their companies have to rethink the way they do business. During the late 1990s especially, BMI has raised significant attention from both practitioners and scholars, considering that it forms a distinct feature in multiple research streams nowadays.

The burgeoning literature stream of business models offers several new fields for management and innovation scholars. Early research was heavily triggered by public attention and the dot-com bubble. Chesbrough and Rosenbloom (2002) are among the first scholars to advance the field by presenting a tangible classification of a business model. They define six functions of a business model, namely *value proposition, market segment, value chain, cost structure and profit potential, value network*, and *competitive strategy*. Influenced by the new economy phenomenon and e-business, a further influential attempt to root the topic of business models in research has been made by Amit and Zott (2001).

Significant advancement in this research field is due to a *Long Range Planning* Special Issue in 2010.[1] A central debate on how to theoretically anchor the business model concept was initiated. Demil and Lecocq (2010), for instance, enquire to what extent the business model is a static or dynamic construct by introducing the *RCOV framework* of business models, which stands for the key components they define, namely resources and competencies, the organization, and value proposition. They find that these elements are in permanent disequilibrium. A firm must possess the capability of *dynamic consistency* to sustain performance while changing its business model. In a different manner, Baden-Fuller and Morgan (2010) explore the detailed meaning of the term *model* in the context of business models by interlinking their research with theories in economics, biology, and philosophy. As a result, the authors regard business models as recipes that have ingredients, such as resources, capabilities, products, customers, technologies, and markets. Zott and Amit (2010) in turn adopt the notion that a business model is an *activity system*. Activity systems comprise activity content, activity system structure, and activity system governance.

Due to the variety of different concepts, an overall theory to explain the phenomenon of business models is still missing. According to Teece (2010), the reason for this might be that the business model has not been thoroughly anchored in traditional management theory and, vice versa—meaning research on business models often lacks a profound theoretical basis. He highlights the need to adopt the business model concept in traditional economic theories, as they too often assume perfect competition, transparent markets, strong property rights, the costless transfer of information, perfect arbitrage, and no innovation. The incorporation of business models into economic theories may radically transform them.

Despite all variation and confusion, business model research has settled on some shared notions on the topic.

First, scholars have come to see that a central advantage of the business model is to draw a holistic picture of the business (Zott, Amit, & Massa, 2010) and explain how the focal firm creates and captures value for itself and its various stakeholders within this ecosystem. In this regard, business models can be referred to boundary-breaking concepts that describe how the focal firm is embedded in and interacts with its surrounding environment (Shafer, Smith, & Linder, 2005; Teece, 2010; Zott & Amit, 2008, 2009). They tell the story of a business by taking into account different components and putting them together as a whole (Chesbrough & Rosenbloom, 2002; Magretta, 2002; Demil & Lecocq, 2010; McGrath, 2010; Morris, Schindehutte, & Allen, 2005; Osterwalder, Pigneur, & Clark, 2010). When it comes to defining these specific key components of a business model, the literature departs (Wirtz, Pistoia, Ullrich & Göttel, 2015). However, many scholars agree on three central themes, namely the value proposition, value creation, and value capture (Doganova & Eyquem-Renault, 2009; Teece, 2010; Tongur & Engwall, 2014).

Second, scholars have widely acknowledged that the business model is a key source of competitive advantage (Baden-Fuller & Morgan, 2010; Björkdahl, 2009; Chesbrough, 2007; Comes & Berniker, 2008; Hamel, 2000; Mitchell & Coles, 2003; Venkatraman & Henderson, 2008), facilitates first-mover advantages (Markides & Sosa, 2013), and may affect firm performance (Afuah, 2004; Afuah & Tucci, 2001).

This, unmistakably, makes the business model a burgeoning unit of analysis in management research albeit the lacking unifying perspective (Foss & Saebi, 2015). Moreover, the concept of business models is not exclusive to one single functional research discipline, such as organizational behaviour, strategy, innovation management, and marketing, and it has to be accepted that it will probably remain a boundary-spanning element in research. However, this theoretical heterogeneity and diversity might even be fruitful to open up the full debate on business models and shed light from different angles. Thus, it would be helpful to observe the business model phenomenon through different theoretical lenses. Consequently, one eclectic theory on business models might emerge in the future. As of now, it is more probable that different angles and perspectives would enrich the debate and leverage the knowledge-creation process in academia as well as know-how development in practice.

NOTE

1. The increase in research has been underlined by the amount of further special issues on business model innovation ever since. Examples are *Strategic Organization* (2013, Volume 11, Issue 4), *International Journal of Innovation Management* (2013, Volume 17, Number 1), *R&D Management* (2014, Volume 44, Issue 3), and *Strategic Entrepreneurship Journal* (2015, Volume 9, Issue 1).

BIBLIOGRAPHY

Afuah, A. (2004). *Business models: A strategic management approach*. Boston: McGraw-Hill.
Afuah, A., & Tucci, C. L. (2001). *Internet business models and strategies*. Boston: McGraw-Hill International Editions.
Amit, R., & Zott, C. (2001). Value creation in e-business. *Strategic Management Journal, 22*, 493–520.
Baden-Fuller, C,, & Morgan, M. S. (2010). Business models as models. *Long Range Planning, 43*(2–3), 156–171.
Björkdahl, J. (2009). Technology cross-fertilization and the business model: The case of integrating ICTs in mechanical engineering products. *Research Policy, 38*(9), 1468–1477.
Chesbrough, H. (2007). Business model innovation: It's not just about technology anymore. *Strategy & Leadership, 35*(6), 12–17.
Chesbrough, H., & Rosenbloom, R. S. (2002). The role of the business model in capturing value from innovation: Evidence from Xerox Corporation's technology spin-off companies. *Industrial and Corporate Change, 11*(3), 529–555.
Comes, S., & Berniker, L. (2008). Business model innovation. In D. Pantaleo & N. Pal (Eds.), *From strategy to execution* (pp. 65–86). Berlin/Heidelberg: Springer.
Demil, B., & Lecocq, X. (2010). Business model evolution: In search of dynamic consistency. *Long Range Planning, 43*(2–3), 227–246.

Doganova, L., & Eyquem-Renault, M. (2009). What do business models do? Innovation devices in technology entrepreneurship. *Research Policy, 38*(10), 1559–1570.

Foss, N. J., & Saebi, T. (2015). Business models and business model innovation. In N. J. Foss & T. Saebi (Eds.), *Business model innovation – The organizational dimension* (pp. 1–23). Oxford: Oxford University Press Inc.

Hamel, G. (2000). *Leading the revolution Harvard Business School Press.* Boston: Harvard Business School Press.

Magretta, J. (2002). Why business models matter. *Harvard Business Review, 80,* 86–87.

Markides, C., & Sosa, L. (2013). Pioneering and first Berlin advantages: The importance of business models. *Long Range Planning, 46*(4–5), 325–334.

McGrath, R. G. (2010). Business models: A discovery driven approach. *Long Range Planning, 43*(2–3), 247–261.

Mitchell, D., & Coles, C. (2003). The ultimate competitive advantage of continuing business model innovation. *Journal of Business Strategy, 24*(5), 15–21.

Morris, M., Schindehutte, M., & Allen, J. (2005). The entrepreneur's business model: Toward a unified perspective. *Journal of Business Research, 58,* 726–735.

Osterwalder, A., Pigneur, Y., & Clark, T. (2010). *Business model generation : A handbook for visionaries, game changers, and challengers.* Hoboken: Wiley.

Shafer, S. M., Smith, H. J., & Linder, J. C. (2005). The power of business models. *Business Horizons, 48,* 199–207.

Teece, D. J. (2010). Business models, business strategy and innovation. *Long Range Planning, 43*(2–3), 172–194.

Tongur, S., & Engwall, M. (2014). The business model dilemma of technology shifts. *Technovation, 34*(9), 525–535.

Venkatraman, N., & Henderson, J. (2008). Four vectors of business model innovation: Value capture in a network ERA. In D. Pantaleo & N. Pal (Eds.), *From strategy to execution* (pp. 259–280). Berlin/Heidelberg: Springer.

Wirtz, B. W., Pistoia, A., Ullrich, S., & Göttel, V. (2015). Business models: Origin, development and future research perspectives. *Long Range Planning, 46,* 36–54.

Zott, C., & Amit, R. (2008). The fit between product market strategy and business model: Implications for firm performance. *Strategic Management Journal, 26,* 1–26.

Zott, C., & Amit, R. (2009). The business model as the engine of network-based strategies. In *The network challenge* (pp. 259–275). Upper Saddle River: Wharton School Publishing.

Zott, C., & Amit, R. (2010). Business model design: An activity system perspective. *Long Range Planning, 43*(2–3), 216–226.

Zott, C., Amit, R., & Massa, L. (2010, September). The business model: Theoretical roots, recent developments, and future research. *IESE Research Papers, 3,* 45.

CHAPTER 2

Leading Business Model Research: The Seven Schools of Thought

Abstract This chapter examines how business model research has been addressed in the past by presenting the seven dominant schools of thought on business models. Each of their theoretical background particularly enables us to understand patterns, causal and logical relationships, as well as processes of business models. By analysing a case from the perspective of each school of thought, the schools are portrayed in a comprehensive manner. In addition, commonalities, overlaps, and differences such as their demarcation from strategy research are discussed. The chapter rounds off in building the bridge to the subsequent chapters of this book and highlighting the role of theories for explaining the phenomenon.

Keywords Review of business model/business model innovation literature • Theoretical background • Realist view • Cognitive view on business models • Business model theories • Business models and strategy • Phenomenon-driven research • Theoretical paradigm shifts

Business model research has been intensified significantly in the last decade. The field seems to have emerged into its own discipline, building on the established areas of strategic management on the one side, and technology and innovation management on the other side. The emergence of business model research into its own discipline can be viewed as an early phase in which different schools are developing and merging. We present a selection of seven research groups that have attained prominence because

© The Editor(s) (if applicable) and the Author(s) 2016
O. Gassmann et al., *Exploring the Field of Business Model Innovation*,
DOI 10.1007/978-3-319-41144-6_2

of their innovative approaches or theoretical input on business models. Before providing a preliminary discussion on the leading business model research, an overview of the seven schools of thoughts is given.

2.1   ACTIVITY SYSTEM SCHOOL (IESE BUSINESS SCHOOL AND WHARTON SCHOOL OF THE UNIVERSITY OF PENNSYLVANIA)

A business model is a set of interdependent activities spanning firm boundaries

The authors define a business model as 'structure, content and governance of transactions' (Zott & Amit, 2008, 2010). Content refers to the selection of activities that are performed to deliver the value proposition. The structure of an activity system refers to how these activities are delivered and interlinked, that is, how the required capabilities, activities, and processes add up to deliver and distribute the value proposition. This dimension thus primarily refers to the organization and architecture of the value chain activities, and 'it also captures their importance for the business model, for example, in terms of their core, supporting or peripheral nature' (p. 220). Ultimately, the activity system's governance defines who performs which activities.

Inherent to this approach, Amit and Zott (2001) undertake a first attempt to link economic theories to the value-creation activities of a business, namely transaction cost economics, Schumpeterian innovation, the resource-based view (RBV), and strategic networks. In doing so, they describe four main sources of value creation anchored in business models with relationships to the renowned economic theories, namely efficiency (transaction cost economics), novelty (Schumpeterian innovation), complementarities (rooted in resource-based theory), and lock-in (strategic networks). By this, they present design themes as the holistic gestalt of a company's activity system and suggest the NICE framework (novelty, lock-in, complementarities, and efficiency).

In addition, they contribute to research on business models by studying the contingency relationship between strategy and structure in order to explore the fit between a business model and product market strategy (Zott & Amit, 2008). Based on previous works, such as Porter (1985) and Lieberman and Montgomery (1988), three product market strategy choices are identified: cost leadership, differentiation, and timing of entry into a market. Their quantitative empirical research yields several contributions.

First, while differentiation and cost leadership are mutually exclusive (or else the 'stuck in the middle' situation emerges), novelty and efficiency are complimentary. Second, the business model and product market strategy have a good fit. Third, the impact that the business model has on the product market strategy is clear and considerable. Fourth, the authors discover that business model design and the development of a product market strategy can occur simultaneously. Nevertheless, the authors argue that not enough research is being undertaken on how a product market strategy and the innovation of a business model coevolve.

Zott and Amit further develop their research on business models by contributing a paper to the *Long Range Planning* Special Issue in 2010 about the different constituent parts of a business model (Zott & Amit, 2010). By building on previous work, they develop the activity system perspective, as depicted in Fig. 2.1. The activity system can be described by design elements and design themes. Design elements characterize the activity system and include the content, structure, and governance of an activity system as noted above. An activity system can also be characterized by design themes, which detail the dominant value creation drivers. The central design themes that connect the elements of an activity system are the following: novelty, lock-in, efficiency, and complementarities.

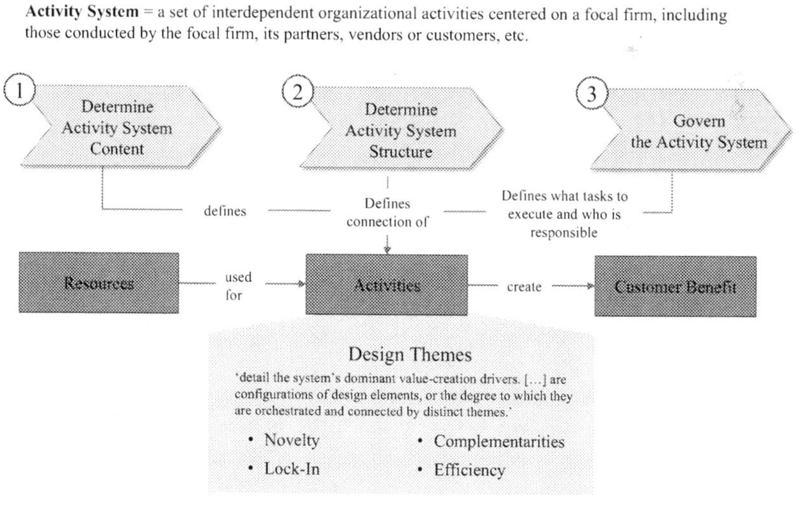

Activity System = a set of interdependent organizational activities centered on a focal firm, including those conducted by the focal firm, its partners, vendors or customers, etc.

Fig. 2.1 Activity system perspective on business models as presented by the research group around Amit and Zott

The research group was enlarged by Massa in 2011, when they released a literature review (Zott, Amit, & Massa, 2011). Four main observations of general consensus are clarified. First, the business model has gradually become a new unit of analysis. Second, the business model emphasizes a system-level, holistic approach towards explaining how firms do business. Third, organizational activities play an important role in the various conceptualizations of business models. Fourth, the business model seeks to explain how value is created and captured. A solid, common conceptual base is still lacking, to which Zott et al. (2011) make two suggestions for improvement. First, the topic of a business model needs more precise constructs upon which all researchers could agree. Second, some researchers perceive business models as a systemic perspective on how to do business, while others see them as sources of value creation. Both interpretations are mutually beneficial. Hence, distinguishing between these views could be a way to structure the topic and provide clarification. It is argued that these two suggestions would improve the research of business models by bringing a conceptual consolidation among researchers throughout the world.

The Activity system school focuses on a thorough theoretical base in business model research. This research group has managed to push a first approach towards a theory of business models. The so-called activity system perspective on business models is a widely accepted framework within academia. It is based on the ideas of integrating aspects from value chain analysis, the RBV, theory of strategic networks, as well as transaction cost economics.[1]

2.2   Process School (IAE Business School)

A business model is a dynamic process of balancing revenue, costs, organization, and value

Demil and Lecocq (2010) stress the importance of dynamics that affect the development of a business model. First, the authors highlight three core components of a business model, namely *resources and competencies*, *organizational structure*, and *propositions for value delivery*. Trying to structure a business model according to these components points to sources of revenues and helps identify cost drivers. By explaining the relationships between the three components and their respective revenue streams and cost structure, the authors develop a framework they

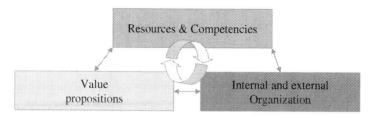

Fig. 2.2   RCOV framework of the process school (Adapted from Demil and Lecocq (2010))

call resources, competencies, organization, and value (RCOV) proposition. Demil and Lecocq (2010) contribute to business model research by pointing out that the relationships between the components are the subject of dynamic change, and that looking at a specific business model at a certain point in time merely provides a snapshot of the current situation. Changes to the model may occur within or between the components. A development *within* is hereby defined as a change of a component that initiates another change in the same component, whereas a change *between* components always affects at least two components. Moreover, the environment can be regarded as an exogenous factor to the RCOV framework with an influence on either of the core components (Fig. 2.2).

In this way, the authors combine the static view on business models, 'which aims to describe the configurations of elements producing (or not) good performance, and the dynamic view, which tries to grasp the ways in which a business model evolves over time' (p. 242). According to the authors, anticipating and reacting to the 'consequences of evolution in any given component' (p. 230) is a capability crucial to build and maintain sustainable firm performance. Moreover, change in a business model might occur on purpose and voluntarily or as an unintended emerging change. These emerging changes can either be positive, such as low interest on borrowings, or negative, initiating vicious circles, like an explosion of salary costs. Hence, even if top management does not purposefully decide to transform the business model, it might still change, thereby affecting elements and core components. Following the authors argument, a business model is, therefore, 'permanently in a state of transitory disequilibrium' (Demil & Lecocq, 2010, p. 240), which means it tries to adapt and aims to eliminate inefficiencies and improve the exploitation of resources.

The research group around Demil & Lecocq, in addition to the introduction of a dynamic perspective of business models, contributes to research by asking whether a business model can be viewed as a research program, a term coined by Lakatos (1971). Lecocq et al. (2010) define a research program as a stream of theories that show certain continuity even if some of the theories are questioned or even contradicted by other observations. Such a research program, therefore, is constituted by a non-falsifiable core around which auxiliary hypotheses form a protective belt. Lecocq et al. (2010) show that research on BMI may be viewed as a 'business model program' (p. 217). The business model program concentrates on certain core assumptions, which distinguish it from other strategic management programs. For example, the focus is 'on the generation of value and revenues and less on the construction of a competitive advantage' (p. 217) or 'the fact that products and organizational architectures are jointly considered and influence each other' (p. 217). Furthermore, the authors name some of the ancillary, protective hypotheses of the program that are debated but not yet accepted as core assumptions. Examples include Maloneetal. (2006), who investigates the 'kind of relationships between the different elements and the various configurations' (Lecocq et al., 2010, p. 218). Through this classification of BMI as a research program, the authors bring greater clarity to the state of the research on business models and provide a useful framework to structure the existing literature.

Demil, Lecocq, and colleagues make two important contributions in business model research. First, Lecocq et al. (2010) attempt to structure the topic of business models and anchor it in economic research by explaining why business models can be seen as a research program. Second, they attempt to point out the importance of pledging a more holistic perspective on the topic by combining the static and dynamic views on business models. They argue that business models are subject to continuous internal and external change and, therefore, are in a permanent state of disequilibrium. Scholars following this research group are thus increasingly following a dynamic capabilities perspective on business models.[2]

2.3   Cognitive School (Cass Business School)

A business model is a 'model' or the 'logic' of how firms do business

The activities of the research group around the author Baden-Fuller are distinguished by a rather cognitive stance. Following the seminal paper *Business models as models* (Baden-Fuller & Morgan, 2010), this research not only regards business models as tangible frameworks or tools but also takes a first step to interpreting business models as both abstract ideal types and story-telling constructs. In this context, business models may serve as imitable blueprints for managers.

In Baden-Fuller and Morgan (2010), the authors suggest opening up the focus and approach business models from outside the subject area of management. The crux of the matter is the term *model*, which has been conceptually rooted in the fields of philosophy, biology, and economics. Stretching the conceptual experiment to adopt notions from different disciplines, the authors consider business models with an approach normally used by, for instance, biologists. To illustrate the point, biologists study laboratory mice not for the point of studying mice but for studying the life form they represent: mammals. By the same logic, one firm can be studied to analyse a *genre* of firms. In another way of interpreting models, the authors point out that since all firms share certain similarities, generic kinds of behaviour can be traced to simplify the analysis (named *scale models*), and *role models*—that is, something to be copied–can be identified. A last proposition is to consider business models as results of recipes: practical models of technology that are ready not only for copying but also for variation and innovation. In this metaphor, the ingredients of those *recipes* would be resources, capabilities, products, customers, technologies, markets, and so on.

The 2010 paper of the research group continues exploiting this theoretical background and builds on former research. For instance, Baden-Fuller and Winter (2007) previously introduce the notion of principles and templates for replicating organizational knowledge within multi-unit firms wherein a template 'is a working example of an organizational process in use, considered as a repository of process knowledge that is potentially subject to copying' (p. 10.) Principles, on the other hand, 'capture knowledge at a deeper level than templates; that is they indicate what factors can produce which anticipated effects, and an appreciation of why' (p. 11). In this same vein, the research group now uses the business model as a central unit of analysis and stresses the possibility of replicating, adopting, or copying business models (Baden-Fuller & Morgan, 2010) (Fig. 2.3).

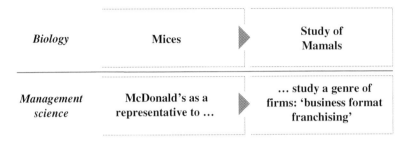

Biology	Mices	▶	Study of Mamals
Management science	McDonald's as a representative to ...	▶	... study a genre of firms: 'business format franchising'

Fig. 2.3 Transferring the idea of 'ideal types to study' onto business models

In a more recent paper, Baden-Fuller and Haefliger (2013) enquire as to how technological innovations and business models are related, and notice that even though both are strongly interlinked, the business model construct is essentially separable from technology. According to the authors, this observation causes confusion among academics and practitioners and needs to be studied more closely by identifying the relationship between business models and technology. A literature review reveals two conclusions. First, using a framework composed of customers, customer engagement, value, delivery, linkages and mone-tization, business models mediate the link between technology and firm performance. Second, 'developing the right technology is a matter of a business model decision regarding openness and user engagement' (p. 419).

> Baden-Fuller and colleagues follow a model-based view on business models and draw on insights from other research disci-plines (e.g. biology, philosophy, and economics). Central to this effort is detecting typologies and taxonomies in the field of busi-ness models. In this regard, they put the entrepreneur or manager and their entrepreneurial pathways of designing business models in the centre of their considerations. In addition, they strive to build a bridge from technology management literature streams to business models.[3]

2.4   TECHNOLOGY-DRIVEN SCHOOL (UNIVERSITY OF CALIFORNIA, BERKELEY)

A business model is a way to commercialize novel technology

The research group around Henry Chesbrough and David J. Teece shares a common ground by exploring the role of the business model in commercializing technology. However, they examine this matter in different but complementary ways. Chesbrough focuses on how to commercialize new technologies primarily by analysing spin-off strategies (Chesbrough & Rosenbloom, 2002; Chesbrough, 2009) and open business models (Chesbrough 2006, 2007b) on the one hand. Teece, on the other hand, draws on the *profiting from innovation framework* (Teece, 2010, 2012) and the role of dynamic capabilities in designing viable business models (Teece, 2010; Leih, Linden, & Teece, 2015). Hence, both authors adapt their very own theoretical background onto the concept of business models: Henry Chesbrough, by focusing on organizational matters and David J. Teece, by adopting the theory of dynamic capabilities. Both streams are presented in the following:

Chesbrough and Rosenbloom (2002) were one of the first to explicitly study business models. In the seminal paper on Xerox's technology spin-offs, they explored the role a business model takes in capturing value from early-stage technology ventures. Chesbrough and Rosenbloom (2002) present six different functions a business model should possess: value proposition, market segment, value chain, cost structure/profit potential, value network, and competitive strategy.

Chesbrough was also one of the first to introduce the concept of *open business models.* Chesbrough (2006, 2007b) proposes that incumbents should open up their traditionally closed business models because a stronger collaboration with partners helps a firm to find and seize novel, external opportunities. Conceptually, the open business model extends the concept of openness from the innovation and value creation context to all aspects of a business model.

In discussing barriers to BMI and open business models, Chesbrough (2010) comes up with qualitative research on potential ways of circumventing the usual internal barriers. To overcome resistance, that is, the *dominant logic,* or the hurdle to focus on entirely new models, the author first notices that discovery-driven planning could model the uncertainties and update financial projections. Second, he points out the relevance of

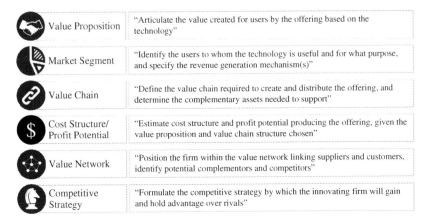

	Value Proposition	"Articulate the value created for users by the offering based on the technology"
	Market Segment	"Identify the users to whom the technology is useful and for what purpose, and specify the revenue generation mechanism(s)"
	Value Chain	"Define the value chain required to create and distribute the offering, and determine the complementary assets needed to support"
	Cost Structure/ Profit Potential	"Estimate cost structure and profit potential producing the offering, given the value proposition and value chain structure chosen"
	Value Network	"Position the firm within the value network linking suppliers and customers, identify potential complementors and competitors"
	Competitive Strategy	"Formulate the competitive strategy by which the innovating firm will gain and hold advantage over rivals"

Fig. 2.4 Business model components according to the Technology-driven school (Adapted from Chesbrough and Rosenbloom (2002, pp. 533–534))

effectual logic to innovating business models, following actions based on initial results of previous experiments (Fig. 2.4).

In order to explore the same research question of how business models may successfully commercialize technology, Teece (2010) draws on the *profiting from innovation framework* as presented in Teece (2006). This framework holds that firms and entrepreneurs may design a business model based on different commercialization strategies which reside on the continuum of highly integrated business models on the one end and pure licensing approaches on the other.

Most importantly, however, Teece (2010) launched a discussion concerning the aspect of dynamics in business models. Scholars have contributed to this vein mainly by drawing on the dynamic capability framework developed by Teece and Pisano (1994) and Teece, Pisano, & Shuen (1997), which provides a process perspective on the development, reconfiguration, and release of internal as well as external resources (Eisenhardt & Martin, 2000). In contrast to an RBV, a dynamic capability framework sheds light on the question of how managers adapt and develop business models in the wake of fast changing external environments (Cavalcante, Kesting, & Ulhoi, 2011). Leih, Linden, and Teece (2015) highlight that 'the successful intertemporal management of value creation, delivery, and capture is a key dynamic capability' for BMI, and that 'certain aspects of organizational design, such as shallow hierarchies and pro-entrepreneurial incentive design, are important supports for dynamic capabilities' (p. 37). In another vein, Achtenhagen, Melin, and Naldi (2013) present three central capabilities, 'an orientation towards experimenting with and exploiting new business opportunities, a balanced use of resources, as well as achieving coherence between leadership, culture, and employee commitment, together shaping key strategizing actions' (p. 431). A deeper understanding on the process perspective on business models is only just emerging, but presents a promising pathway for future research.

Ultimately, both authors of the research group reach to the conclusion that a business model is not a strategy, since a good deal of managers confuse the two terms. Business models should create value for the customer and, thus, the model is constructed around delivering that value. Chesbrough and Rosenbloom (2002) present two business model goals, which are subtly different from those of a strategy. First, a business model should directly indicate how a business creates value. Second, whereas a strategy requires careful, analytic calculation and choice, a business model consciously assumes that knowledge is cognitively limited and biased by the earlier success of the firm. The cognitive implication derived from the defining characteristics is that a business model links the technical physical domain to the economic domain. Unlike the physical domain, which is typically well defined with hard facts and observations, the economic domain is filled with vague and unclear variables, facts, and questions. Hence, there is a cost of structuring a business model, which is the filtering out of certain possibilities due to cognitive limitation and bias imposed by the business model itself. Teece (2010), in a similar vein, highlights that the business model is a more generic concept than a strategy as selecting a strategy 'is a more granular exercise than designing a business model' (p. 180). Thus, a through strategic analysis builds the ground for every sustainable business model design.

The research group is interested in building the bridge to technology management. Chesbrough focuses on the aspects of spin-off strategies and open business models, and thus explores organizational matters. Teece is interested in exploring the role of dynamic capabilities for BMI. Both highlight the demarcation of the concept of business models from strategic management research.[4]

2.5   Strategic Choice School (Harvard Business School)

A business model is a result of strategic choices

Enriching the ongoing debate on how business model and strategy are interlinked, Casadesus-Masanell and Ricart (2010b) attempt to clarify the differentiation as well as the gap between strategy and tactics. The authors underline not only the lack of a clear distinction but also the fact that most managers confuse these three concepts: strategy, business model, and tactic, and that academics have not been doing enough to clarify the gaps. The authors explain that business models are results of strategic decisions. Once a business model is employed, a firm makes tactical decisions within the well-defined rules of play constrained by the chosen business model. In this regard, strategic business model choices are the most complex task for firms. First, the rules of the game are usually not well defined. Second, the mapping of potential strategic outcomes dependent on different choice scenarios is extremely complicated, as each modification of the strategy requires a full re-assessment of the tactics. Third, it is impossible to predict the competing firms' reactions on a strategic level.

Apart from their conceptual research on business models, Casadesus-Masanell and Ricart (2010a) expose the relationship between competitiveness and the concept of business models based on case studies. The

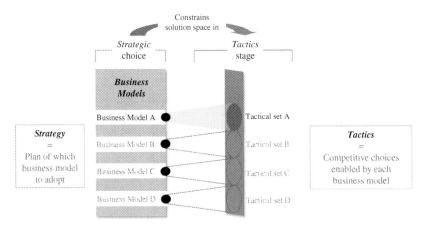

Fig. 2.5 Perspective on business models as presented by the strategic choice school (Adapted from Casadesus-Masanell and Ricart (2010a))

authors argue that if managers aim to gain a sustainable competitive advantage in an efficient way, they should shift their focus to their business model, since it sits at the very core of competitiveness. In addition, the authors point out the need for firms to innovate their business models at every perceptible and noticeable change in their market environment. Thus, they expose the interaction between business models and changes in the environment (Fig. 2.5).

The Strategic choice school also finds that business models may serve as blueprints and are subjects for imitation. Casadesus-Masanell and Zhu (2013) empirically explore this topic in a formal analysis of strategic interactions between innovative entrants and incumbents building on profit functions as unit of analysis. In their study, which builds on elements of game theory, the incumbent 'may imitate the entrant's business model once revealed' (p. 464). This research yields interesting conclusions. First, given that it is possible for incumbents to imitate and copy the entrant's novel business model, the entrants should either (1) 'strategically choose (whether) to reveal their innovation by competing through the new business model' or (2) conceal their innovation by adopting the traditional business model. From the incumbent's perspective, depending on the environment, the BMI brought by the new entrant may be so valuable and substantial 'that an incumbent may prefer to compete in a duopoly rather than to remain a monopoly' (p. 464).

> The research group around Casadesus-Masanell pursues the connection between business models and existent streams of theory in strategic management. The theoretical triangle of competitive imitation literature, competitive advantages, and game theory builds the framework for several papers.[5]

2.6   RECOMBINATION SCHOOL (UNIVERSITY OF ST. GALLEN)

A business model is a recombination of patterns for answering the who–what–how–why questions of a business

Gassmann, Frankenberger, and Csik (2014) suggest a framework that structures a business model in four dimensions, namely the customer, the value proposition, the value chain dimension, and the revenue model.

They define the cornerstones of business models as answers to the following four questions.

1. *Who?* Every business model serves a certain customer group (Hamel, 2000). Thus, it should answer the question 'Who is the customer?' (Magretta, 2002).
2. *What?* The second dimension describes what is offered to the customer, or put differently, what the customer values. This notion is commonly referred to as the value proposition (Teece, 2010).
3. *How?* To build and distribute the value proposition, a firm has to master several processes and activities. These processes and activities go along with the involved resources (Hedman & Kalling, 2003) and capabilities (Morris et al., 2005).
4. *Why?* Why does the business model generate profit or, more generally, value? This dimension explains why the business model is financially viable, and therefore relates to the revenue model. In essence, it unifies aspects, such as cost structure and revenue mechanisms.

The core philosophy of the research team builds on an extensive study of the vast majority of all successfully developed business models over the past 50 years plus a number of pioneering ones from the past 150 years. The central finding is that 90 per cent of all business models are built on the basis of 55 repetitive patterns. This research approach to BMI is in line with other current endeavours which try to develop archetypes, categorizations, or morphologies in BMI. In a more theoretical manner, this view on business models builds on such scholars as Baden-Fuller and Morgan (2010) and Doganova and Eyquem-Renault (2009). These studies highlight the fact that business models may act as a blueprint or template and regard BMI activities as a form of imitation. Thus, the central innovation mechanism is the fusion of and building on existing knowledge to drive new business models. In addition, the use of analogies for creative imitation has been acknowledged as a source of innovation in traditional innovation management literature (Hargadon, 2002). By having their empirical findings embedded in a methodology, those business model patterns can be applied to design new business models in practice. In addition, the methodology was inspired by the 'theory of inventive problem solving' stemming from the discipline of mechanical engineering. Hence, their approach may be best located in competitive imitation and innovation process literature streams.

Value Creation and Value Capture

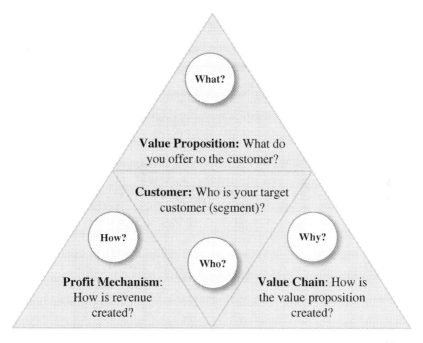

Fig. 2.6   The 'Magic Triangle' of the recombination school

Another central point of this research group is open business models. Frankenberger, Weiblen, and Gassmann (2013) are among the first to apply a network theory perspective on the concept of open business models. A central result of this research is the derivation of three archetypes of network configurations for solution providers that use open business models. Depending on the level of customer centricity, a company aims for different levels of openness, and distinct network configurations are suggested accordingly (Fig. 2.6).

Frankenberger, Weiblen, and Gassmann (2014) further explore their research on open business models by analysing the antecedents of this specific type of business model. In a multi-case analysis of eight incumbent companies that apply open business models, five types of antecedents are found, namely business model inconsistency, the need to create and capture value, previous experience with collaboration, open business model patterns, and industry convergence. The same study suggests differentiation of open business models in four types of openness (structured by the two dimensions of *dependence of openness* and *locus of openness*).

> Gassmann's research group pioneers in translating an engineering science theory—the theory of inventive problem solving, in mechanical engineering more commonly known as TRIZ—to management science. The approach can be rooted in creativity research as well as competitive imitation. The group also contributes to academic research by analysing open business models and applying network theory.[6]

2.7   Duality School (London Business School)

A business model does coexist with competing business models and requires ambidextrous thinking

The contribution of this research group to the area of business models is threefold. First, the term BMI is theoretically demarcated from radical product and technological innovations. Second, it tackles the topic of managing dual business. Third, the business model is interlinked with the topic of ambidexterity, which is the capability to balance two types of learning behaviour–*exploitation* and *exploration*. Apart from the theoretical contribution and conceptual far-sightedness, this research also includes BMI for emerging markets.

Markides (2006) enquires how BMI is a distinct phenomenon compared to technological innovations and new-to-the-world product innovations. He proposes treating them individually, as they produce different kinds of markets and have different managerial implications. For instance, new business models 'are not necessarily superior to the ones established companies employ, a fact implying that it is not necessarily an optimal strategy for an established company to abandon its existing business model in favour of something new or to grow the new model alongside its existing business model' (p. 21). BMIs are characterized, for instance, by approaching new customer groups or by significantly extending an existing customer base. BMIs redefine the core product or service and emphasize different attributes of the same. Thus, they are rather radical (Markides, 2006).

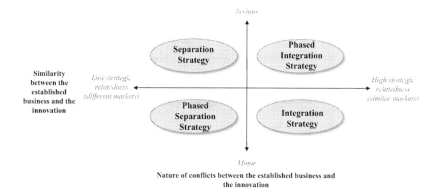

Fig. 2.7 Different strategies for managing dual business models (Adapted from Markides and Charitou (2004, p. 24))

According to the Duality school, implementing a novel business model requires explorative activities as BMIs are somehow new in nature and long for new organizational processes, structures, and capabilities. This stays in stark contrast to an operating business model of a company, which is most often directed at exploitation. A conflict emerges which is characterized by whether there is a conflict with the established business and whether there is a similarity with the established business as depicted in Fig. 2.7. Based on these two dimensions, the Duality school suggests several organizational mechanisms (Markides & Charitou, 2004).

Research on managing dual business models is somewhat congruent and mutually enriching, especially if one considers the publications that interlink BMI with ambidexterity. Dual business models refer to competing with more than one, and potentially cannibalizing, business models in a single market. There is a considerable body of research that argues in favour of structural separation when it comes to such a form of BMI. This implies a complete separation of activities. Markides (2013), however, argues that this approach might fall too short and a more differentiated picture has to be drawn. The 2013 paper calls for refining this view (Markides, 2013). For instance, it encourages exploring how other modes of ambidexterity, namely contextual and temporal ambidexterity, might be beneficial for the implementation and management of BMI.

The Duality school takes the organizational dimension of BMI into consideration. More specifically, it focuses on managing parallel business models by interlinking BMI with literature on organizational ambidexterity. An additional aspect central to their research is the topic of resource constraint innovation and business models for emerging markets. Although the research is thoroughly anchored in theory, it has strong practical implications.[7]

2.8   Case Study: Nespresso from the Perspective of the Seven Schools of Thought

To provide a practical explanation of the presented business model literature, we show how the seven schools of thought refer to a case example. We opted for the Nespresso case since a well-known example eases the understanding of a complex theoretical matter. Moreover, we have selected the case of Nespresso because it has created a major revolution in the coffee business.

One of the most admired BMIs can be traced back to this case. Nespresso successfully managed to transform low-priced commodity coffee into a premium good. At the same time, by combining coffee manufacturing and machine production, the brand is now able to control its entire ecosystem from coffee bean sourcing to producing and selling packaged coffee.

When Nestlé launched Nespresso in 1986, it was confronted with fierce competition in the coffee market due to dominating coffee distributers as well as machine manufacturers. The product has been first developed for a niche market: coffee in offices where the price elasticity of demand is rather low, convenience seemed to be more important than price. Within the past few years, the brand has experienced substantial growth, and Nespresso currently represents the fastest growing business unit of its parent company. The main profit formula lies in the application of a razor and blade model. Nespresso profits not from selling its coffee machines but from the sales of the separate capsules, which have an estimated gross margin of 85 per cent (Conley, Bican, & Ernst, 2013). Nespresso has further managed to accelerate growth by creating emotional value articulation through marketing initiatives such as the Nespresso Club, the fancy design of Nespresso boutiques, and advertisements starring Hollywood celebrity George Clooney.

An Activity system perspective: Starting with the activity system perspective, we elaborate first on the activity system's content, structure, and governance and second on the NICE framework of Nespresso. As noted, **content** refers to the selection of activities that are performed to deliver the value proposition. In the case of Nespresso, these are the constant research and development of the integrated capsule system, the production of the machines and ingredients (including the capsules), the convenient product, service and consumable delivery to the customer, the assurance of unchanging quality and giving the customer an experience of luxurious lifestyle. With regard to the **structure** of Nespresso's activity system, the focus lies in how these activities are delivered and interlinked. This dimension thus primarily refers to the organization and architecture of the value chain activities. Nespresso's activity system structure is coined by a high integration of know-how and activities in the machine and ingredient (coffee) development, the careful and lean coffee supply management, and avoiding the use of intermediaries. Ultimately, the activity system's **governance** defines who performs which activities. For instance, Nespresso distributes the products itself by means of a direct selling model using boutique stores and an own E-commerce platform. Nespresso also produces the capsules and the ingredients itself. Conversely, Nespresso collaborates with *DeLonghi, Krupp,* or *Koenig* in the production of machines. In analysing the design themes, which depict the activity system's dominant value creation drivers, Nespresso mainly focuses on **Novelty** and **Lock-In**. The activity system has created an entirely new customer experience by decoupling the sales activities from regular retailing (novelty). In terms of Lock-in, Nespresso has achieved a high level of protection for the interface by the use of patents. The coffee filter for instance has been integrated in the capsule, which aims to impede imitation (Lock-in).

> *Nespresso's value drivers are located in the two design themes 'Lock-In' (integrated capsule system) and 'Novelty' (Nespresso was one of the first to disentangle sales activities from classic retailing).*

A Process school perspective: A primary focus of the process school is to analyse the dynamic evolution and adaptation of a business model in the wake of external or internal changes. According to the process school, a continual alignment between resources and competencies, the value proposition as well as changes in the internal and external environment has to be achieved. Analysing Nespresso, the business model underwent several stages since its launch in 1986. Nespresso was the first company to pioneer the portioned, encapsulated coffee market. At the beginning they aimed towards a product for professional customers in the offices not for the private households. Activities have also been focused on the core technology, quality, and functional excellence of the product. Later the capability of introducing and managing an innovative revenue model became central and ultimately the brand management became increasingly important. From 1989 on, capsules were delivered to households by mail. In detecting the opportunity of online channels, Nespresso was then the first market player to identify the potential of E-commerce and offered an online-shop in 1996. In the beginning, Nespresso primarily focused on the convenience aspect. With increasing competition in the premium coffee market and capsule technology, the brand management and emotionalization of the value proposition emerged as a central paradigm. However, the patenting activity keeps being an ongoing core capability.

> *Nespresso succeeds with the capability of continuously adapting the business model to novel opportunities such as the need for convenience, the emergence of online sales or the desire for luxurious lifestyle.*

A Cognitive school perspective: According to the cognitive school, BMI combines the copying of scaling models and the adaptation of business role models by managers. For instance, the Cognitive school would differentiate between product- and service-oriented or between network-centric and dyadic models (as noted previously, Nespresso offers a servitized product, produced in a conventional value chain network). Apart from such categorizations, the cognitive school analyses the notion of a business model on an individual level. Therefore, the cognitive school investigates questions of how managers at Nespresso came to innovate their business model. This, for instance, raises the question of how the pathway of entrepreneurial activity took place, asking 'How did managers at Nestlé detect and seize the opportunity to innovate a business model in the absence of any exogenous change?' A key argument of the cognitive school is that business model innovators must overcome an inertia of extant business model schemas.

In doing so, innovators adapt cognitive mechanisms that recombine extant solutions and models in completely new ways by the process of analogical reasoning or conceptual recombination (Martins et al., 2015).

> *Cognitive processes in the minds of Nespresso's entrepreneurs such as 'analogical reasoning' or 'conceptual recombination' triggered the BMI.*

A Technology-driven school perspective: The core product, portioned and encapsulated coffee, was developed by Nestlé in 1986. For a long time, the potential of commercializing that technology remained unexplored. In the words of the Technology-driven school, the epicentre of innovative activities was the technology but only a viable business model drove fulminant success. Indeed, sales significantly picked up as Nespresso directed its attention towards the innovative Razor and Blade business model. From a Technology school's perspective, the capsula was the new technological product which needs to be commercialized in a holistic way. According to this school the business model can be described based on six dimensions: Nespresso offers a **value proposition** of convenient usage and low upfront investment for the customer (a conventional coffee machine usually costs much more than the Nespresso machine). Moreover, Nespresso initially focused on a clear customer group–hip, wealthy, and urban professionals. This led to the creation of an entirely new **market segment** back then–the premium coffee sector. As noted in the activity system perspective, the value chain activities are coined by a high degree of integration of ingredient and hardware in terms of R&D, a direct selling model, and strategic partnerships in production. In terms of the **cost structure/profit potential,** Nespresso has leveraged the integrated technological interface of machine and capsule in a revenue model that lowered the investment costs for a coffee machine significantly. Conversely, the capsules were sold at high prices. The value network of Nespresso is coined by strategic partnerships with machine producers or certified coffee suppliers. Most importantly, Nespresso aims at a position in isolation of competitors or other complementors. Ultimately, the **competitive strategy** of Nespresso is to maintain the monopolistic position in the premium coffee sector, for instance, by increasingly emotionalizing the brand and the value proposition.

The Nespresso capsule technology has been left unused for a long time. Success kicked in as an innovative business model was executed.

A Strategic choice school perspective: The Strategic choice school interlinks business models with the strategic stage (choice of a business model the firm will compete with) and the tactical stage (residual choices a firm can make on the basis of the chosen business model). A business model is thus composed of two elements-concrete choices by the management on the business model and the respective constraints and consequences of this choice. Moreover, the Strategic choice school analyses if and how incumbents change their business model once new entrants arise or competitors change their business model. Some distinctive features and choices of Nespresso's business model are to eliminate intermediaries, sell consumables at high margins, sell machines at low margins, integrate the interface between capsule and machine, and pursue a high-pricing strategy. Resulting consequences of this business model choice is Nespsresso's dependency on revenues based on consumables, the need to maintain a monopolistic position and to attract consumers with relatively high incomes. Competitors soon entered the premium coffee market with similar capsule systems, such as *Cafissimo*, or copied the Nespresso capsules, such as *Denner*. Today there are 85 competitors active - only in the European market. Such competitive imitations are a logical implication according to the Strategic choice school and subsequent actions of the competing firms may be explained by game-theoretical considerations. However, Nespresso did not change its business model to counteract competitors and new entrants. The company rather built on tactical choices to strengthen the extant business model. This included protecting the interface of capsule with machine or the various measures to emotionalize the value proposition in order to attract young urban professionals.

Nespresso opted for a business model based on selling expensive consumables and cheap machines. Consequently, Nespresso necessarily has to maintain a monopolistic position. Nespresso accomplishes this based on a stringent IP management and by emotionalizing the value proposition for instance. These are tactical choices which do not change the overall Nespresso business model.

A **Recombination school perspective:** According to the Recombination school, Nespresso's business model can be described based on four dimensions. This framework explicitly places the customer in the centre of the business model. The so-called **Who** dimension depicts the customer with his pains, needs, and gains. Among these are the high investment costs of an automatic coffee machine such as *Jura*. Nespresso has also come to see that a critical pain-point for customer loyalty was the break-down of a machine. In order to increase robustness and lengthen the lifespan of a machine, Nespresso fitted the gasket into the capsules for instance. The **What** dimension depicts how this technical solution has been integrated into a convenient value proposition. Subsequently, the **How** dimension shows how Nespresso creates and delivers the value proposition to the customer. This dimension thus describes how Nespresso integrates activities of machine and ingredient development, collaborates with strategic supply chain partners in the production of the machines, and so on. Ultimately, the **Why** dimension answers the question of why the business model is profitable and directs the focus on the Razor and blade model, one of the generic business model patterns Nespresso adopts. First, Nespresso adopted the **Razor and blade** model with the core logic being the sales of the basic product (the machine) at low margins and the consumables (the capsules) at high prices. Second, Nespresso applied a **Lock-in** model, whereby companies capture customers in one product segment, increasing switching costs to other systems. Third, the company uses a **Direct selling** pattern, where intermediaries and retailers are discarded. Ultimately, Nespresso adopts the **Customer experience** pattern, by emotionalizing the entire value proposition. In the case of Nespresso this has been achieved by hiring George Clooney as brand ambassador or building boutique stores in fancy shopping promenades (see Gassmann et al. (2014) for an additional case analysis). All business model patterns have been already available from past examples in other industries. For instance, the Razor and blade such as Lock-in pattern have already been adopted by *Gilette* in 1904. The Direct selling pattern has been applied by *Tupperware* for kitchen and household products in the late 1940s and 1950s.

The Nespresso business model is a recombination of the Razor and blade, Lock-in, Direct selling, and Customer experience pattern.

A Duality school perspective: In analysing the Nespresso case, the duality school puts a specific focus on how Nestlé has managed to adopt a second, cannibalizing business model in parallel to the extant Nescafe business model. Nescafe has been the primary business model for selling coffee to the mass market. The instant coffee has been sold based on a retailing structure. Prices were defined at a cost-plus method. As noted in the previous sections, the Nespresso business model differs in nearly all dimensions from conventional business models in the coffee industry. Markides and Charitou (2004) have analysed the implementation of the additional business model and came to see that 'Nespresso coffee was in effect cannibalizing the sales of Nescafe, and the values and attitudes of the Nespresso organization were the exact opposite of those in the traditional Nestle organization' (p. 25). Consequently, Nestlé succeeded in completely separating the novel business model in a new organization that was also geographically separated. According to the Duality school, this seems reasonable as there has been a 'serious conflict between the established business and the business model innovation', and there has been a great 'similarity between the established business and the innovation' (p. 24). It is recalled that great autonomy and freedom were two of the success factors for the implementation of the novel business model (see Markides and Charitou (2004) for an additional case analysis).

> *Nestlé managed conflicting business models (Nescafe vs. Nespresso), by implementing the new business model in a separated organization.*

2.9   Preliminary Discussion

After 25 years of research, the business model literature might be a young field compared to strategic management but a lot of rigorous scholarly work is done. We have presented the seven most comprehensive schools of thought spearheading this field. These represent prominent streams towards a thorough theoretical perspective on business models. Evidently, not all schools are equally acknowledged in research yet. We may, for instance, assert that the activity system perspective is one of the frequently used frameworks in academia. This is probably due to the publications in highly ranked journals and introduction of concepts and measures like novelty- versus efficiency-centred business models. Another much noticed school of thought is the cognitive school, which does a thorough job in demarcating the business model concept in relation to the field of strategic management. However, more important than a discussion about the impact of a school from today's perspective is the assertion that all schools have great potential to further spearhead the field of business models.

Looking at these schools, we may notice some differences, overlaps, or even commonalities in some respects (see Table 2.2).

Starting with the commonalities among the schools, all seven focus on the central question as to how firms create and capture value. A key argument of business model scholars is that the concept of business models has a greater explanatory power compared to previously adopted concepts in strategic management research. For instance, the business model adopts a perspective on firms that is boundary-spanning and explains how the focal firm is embedded in and transacts with its surrounding ecosystem (Shafer, Smith, & Linder, 2005; Teece, 2010; Zott & Amit, 2008, 2009). By modelling the boundaries of the firm and the interface between the company and customers, business models extend the locus of attention compared to classic strategy research. In this vein, all schools of thought give impetus on the emerging concept of joint value creation. Continuing further this line of reasoning, all schools search for a demarcation from the field of strategic management or justification in the field of strategic management, albeit in different ways (see Table 2.1).

In targeting the anchoring of business models in academia, the majority of works presented by these schools still follow a rather conceptual or qualitative perspective, which marks a further commonality among the schools. This is, however, characteristic to the emergence of a research field and potential theory. A rigorous and direct focus on the performance link of a business model choice or novelty of a business model is only subject of analysis for the activity and the strategic choice school (Table 2.2).

One of the biggest issues in the current emergence of a shared notion on business models is its differing usage in various disciplines/research fields such as technology and innovation management, entrepreneurship, or strategic management. Those adopt the notion of a business model in tailored ways. Consequently, different levels of abstraction are presented (e.g. activity systems vs. narratives), and different research foci are adopted (e.g. dual business models of incumbents vs. business models of entrepreneurial firms). These differences have led to a broad range of viewpoints and interpretations, which clearly demarcates a school from the other. Also, some schools of thought adopt a rather static perspective such as the activity system schools, while others are inherently more dynamic in their theoretical underpinning (e.g. the process school).

Table 2.1   Relation of the business model to strategy research

	Demarcation from 'strategy'
Activity system school	The notion of business models as activity systems puts forward a new understanding of firm boundaries and broadens the scope of a 'focal firm', considering it as a network of activities, including external resources. The business model is thus a new unit of analysis in strategy research. The school has for instance explored novelty versus efficiency-centred business models with regard to the product/market strategy of a firm
Process school	The school provides a dynamic view on strategy, opposing the view that competitive advantages must be protected ('i.e. there should be no major changes in an operating BM' (p. 244) and avoiding the drawbacks of hypercompetition theory (Demil & Lecocq, 2010))
Cognitive school	The business model focuses on the interface between a firm and its customers. This specific focus has been mostly neglected in strategic management research. Moreover, the research on cognitive business model schemas differentiates the research from the classic strategy literature
Technology-driven school	The school argues that a business model 'formulates the competitive strategy by which the innovating firm will gain and hold advantage over rivals'. The business model differs from strategy in several ways. 'Firstly, the business model starts by creating value for the customer, and constructs the model around delivering that value (...) A second difference lies in the creation of value for the business, versus creation of value for the shareholder. (...) A final difference (...) lies in the assumptions made about the state of knowledge held by the firm, its customers and third parties.' (Chesbrough & Rosenbloom, 2002, p. 534ff)
Strategic choice school	'Strategy refers to the choice of business model through which the firm will compete'. The business model refers to the logic of the firm, the way it operates, and how it creates value for its stakeholders' (Casadesus-Masanell & Ricart, 2010a, b, p. 196)
Recombination school	Strategy refers to the choice of business model patterns from other industries which will be adapted to the own industry
Duality school	A business model is deeply linked with strategy; a clear demarcation is not drawn explicitly. Competing with dual business models implies pursuing two strategies simultaneously

Table 2.2 Comparison of schools of thought on business models

	Activity system school	Process school	Cognitive school	Technology-driven school	Strategic choice school	Recombination school	Duality school
Maxim	A business model is a set of interdependent activities spanning firm boundaries	A business model is a dynamic process of balancing revenue, costs, organization, and value	A business model is a 'model' or the 'logic' of how firms do business	A business model is a way to commercialize novel technology	A business model is a result of strategic choices	A business model is a recombination of patterns for answering the who–what–how–why questions of a business	A business model coexists with competing business models and requires ambidextrous thinking
Research focus	Configuration of the firm's architecture and its network of exchange partners. Mostly entrepreneurial firms	Adaptation of the business model and its constituting elements to its external environment	Individual and collective minds	Embeddedness of a novel technology into a viable business model	Business model configuration to achieve competitive advantage. Both incumbents and entrepreneurial firms	Business model patterns	Organizational design of dual business models, mostly incumbents
Level of abstraction	Activity systems	Firm-level choices and meta models	Mental models and narratives	Key components	Firm-level choices and meta models	Key components and archetypes	Firm-level choices and meta models

(continued)

Table 2.2 (continued)

	Activity system school	Process school	Cognitive school	Technology-driven school	Strategic choice school	Recombination school	Duality school
Dominant theoretical perspective	Complexity and system dynamics oriented theories, value networks, transaction cost economics, resource-based view, Schumpeterian innovation	Dynamic capabilities, resource-based view	Interpretative theories such as managerial cognition or strategic/cognitive groups and dominant logics	Disruption, Schumpeterian innovation, dynamic capabilities	Game theory, competitive imitation	Creativity theory, competitive imitation, network theory	Organizational ambidexterity
Dynamic perspective	Activities are resources in use; moreover, an activity system is a 'system that is made up of components, linkages between the components, and *dynamics*' (Afuah & Tucci, 2001, p. 4)	Entrepreneurial business model development and business model evolution	Analysis of the pathway of entrepreneurial behaviour	Business model design in the wake of technological disruption	Strategic business model choice (long-term) versus tactical business model adaptation (short-term)	Business model innovation processes	Coexistence of conflicting business models during implementation and over time

	Activity system school	Process school	Cognitive school	Technology-driven school	Strategic choice school	Recombination school	Duality school
Empirical base	Both conceptual and quantitative publications play a significant role in the research. Quantitative approaches for instance focused on analysing a range of 300 Internet-enabled business models. The research is mostly focused on entrepreneurial firms	The work is of a qualitative and conceptual nature. They build on the theoretical work of Lakatos (1971), as well as the Penrosian view of the firm (Penrose, 1960). For their study on business model evolution, they draw on the case of the English football club Arsenal FC	The research group typically follows a qualitative approach on business models using case studies, supplemented by strong conceptual papers on the topic	The most popular case study is certainly their pioneering study on technology-based Xerox spin-offs (Chesbrough & Rosenbloom, 2002)	Research is directed at quantitative, mathematical methods, as well as case studies. A big empirical base was built on a dataset of sponsor-based business models	A major focus is set on profound qualitative case studies and on an analysis of almost all successful business model innovations in the last 50 years. The research is focused on incumbents and entrepreneurial firms	The research group delivers valuable theoretical and conceptual contributions on business models. Further research is mainly based on case studies

This heterogeneity may, however, support the emergence of one eclectic theory on business models. The analysis reveals some fruitful overlaps where the schools may complement each other. For instance, the Process school explores the continuous internal and external adaptation such as dynamic development of the business model. In the sense of Teece (2010) and the Technology-driven school, this would require the capability of sensing, seizing, and transforming business opportunities into financially viable business models as presented by Teece, Pisano, & Shuen (1997). Moreover, the Recombination school explores generic business model patterns and is thus strongly interlinked with how the Cognitive school grasps a business model, namely as a recipe, blueprint, or template. For instance, the Cognitive school introduces the concepts of analogical reasoning and conceptual recombination to innovate a business model (Martins et al., 2015). These two concepts are very familiar with the Recombination school which presents the concept of similarity and confrontation principle (Gassmann et al., 2014). Innovating a business model by the use of the similarity principle means to extract core challenges of your competitive environment. Based on a systematic search and analysis for solutions in related industries, these may be transferred to the own industry logic (this refers to 'analogical reasoning' presented by the Cognitive school). In contrast, the confrontation principle takes an outside-in perspective where the business model is confronted with solutions that are cognitively distant and unrelated (this refers to 'conceptual recombination' presented by the Cognitive school). Also, the Strategic choice school is conceptually interlinked with the Recombination school, as it analyses how generic business (revenue) model patterns are being adapted by firms in order to achieve superior firm performance. The merging and combination of different schools of thought is thus a viable avenue for future research. For instance, the entire process of how a business model, which resides as a schema in an entrepreneur's head (Cognitive school), unfolds in a dynamic implementation process (Process school) and ultimately results in an activity system (Activity system school), has not been sufficiently explored. Combining various viewpoints might enrich the debate on business models and potentially lead to one eclectic picture.

To conclude with another commonality, all schools explicitly draw on renowned management theories, albeit very different theoretical foundations. For example, the Activity systems school adapts Schumpeterian innovation, value networks, transaction cost economics, or the RBV, and thus draws on a broad array of theories. The process school in contrast is hooked on one single dimension, the dynamic capability perspective.

Building on these insights, the 50 theories offered in the next chapter make several contributions. First, we present the different theories which have been adopted by the different schools of thought already. Second, we present additional theories to the ones adopted by the schools. In this regard, we show avenues to theoretically enrich existing schools or even trigger future schools. Third, the collection of theories gives researchers an idea on how far the business model provides significant explanatory power for a phenomenon at all. The concept of the business model has been overestimated or misused many times. Markides (2013), for instance, has shown that much of the work on business models tries to reinvent the wheel without that being required. Consequently, the business model perspective might not provide enough novelty. The author reveals that many questions on business models may be framed as a theoretical challenge. In this way, an extant theory may already provide answers to a phenomenon without having to adopt a business model perspective. Oftentimes, the business model is, in fact, only a way to reframe and relabel something that has already been investigated, which raises the question of the value added by a business model perspective. The 50 theories we present in the next section are one way to elaborate in this important matter.

Before presenting the 50 theories and their correlation to business model research, we conclude by aggregating the seven schools of thought. Earlier attempts to organize literature on business models have adopted several dimensions for that. Wirtz, Pistoia, Ulrich, and Göttel (2015) decomposed business model literature in a stream following a strategic, an organizational and a technology-oriented stance. Massa and Tucci (2014) have delved into the various conceptualizations of business models, and argue that 'these could be structured into several levels of decomposition with varying depth and complexity depending on the degree to which they abstract from the reality they aim to describe' (p. 431). In another vein, Martins, Rindova, and Greenbaum (2015) have recently suggested a subdivision of the current business model research into rational, cognitive, and evolutionary streams. In the rational stream, business models are regarded as 'purposefully designed systems that reflect rational managerial choices and their operating implications' (p. 101). In the evolutionary view, it is argued that changes in business models are triggered by external uncertainty. By engaging in experimentation, managers ultimately find a system of activities to compete effectively. In the cognitive view, it is argued that 'business models reflect managerial mental models, or schemas' (p. 102). Ultimately, Baden-Fuller and colleagues differentiate between a realist view and a conceptual-principled view.

Building on these categorizations, we derive two relevant dimensions for structuring the seven schools as characterized in Fig. 2.8 in a comprehensive overview. The first dimension being the realist versus the cognitive view and the second dimension being the degree of abstraction, adapted from Massa and Tucci (2014):

The degree of abstraction defines whether a business model captures the firm by means of activities, a combination of generic patterns (archetypes), a structural template (key components), and so on. On the lower levels, a business model can be described as a system of interdependent activities or as a system of interdependent choices and their consequences as done by the Activity system school or the Strategic choice school. A higher level conceptualization of a business model can be achieved by adopting key components. This goes along with the widely known business model canvas of Alex Osterwalder, which structures a business model into nine building blocks, namely value proposition, key resources, activities, and partners on the upstream side, customer relationships, channels, and segments on the downstream side,

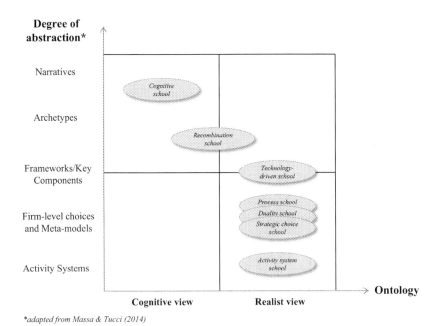

Fig. 2.8   Classification of the seven schools of thought (qualitative)

and ultimately, the cost structure and revenue streams (Osterwalder et al., 2010). Many schools of thought integrate a similar perspective such as the Technology-driven school or the Recombination school. Ultimately, a business model can be grasped as a narrative or a mental model, which reveals a very high level of abstraction, a concept adopted by the Cognitive school.

The second dimension refers to the ontological stance of a business model. An often-shared notion is to differentiate between a realist and a cognitive view. The Activity system school, for instance, adopts a realistic view by depicting and describing individual activities and putting them into a broader business context. Business models are seen as real things that can be formally modelled. In a different attempt, business models can be grasped more informally as mental models or narratives and thus a cognitive phenomenon. A concept adopted by the Cognitive school. Consequently, the business model resides in the head entrepreneurs or managers and guides their actions/entrepreneurial activities/decisions. The higher the degree of abstraction, the more a business model is grasped as a cognitive construct.

As noted before, these seven schools reveal overlaps and mutual influences which points to fruitful pathways of future research.

2.10   ROLE OF THEORIES FOR EXPLAINING A PHENOMENON

Why do we need theories to embed the phenomenon of business models? Business models and the process of BMI are phenomena. Research examines logical and root cause relationships in order to understand an empirical phenomenon, its patterns, and mechanisms, as well as its success factors. Building on this, the business model as a conceptually distinct construct may provide theories with new explanatory power and reach. In this vein, managers can be given tools to lead and manage better.

Generally, a theory is nothing more than a tool to explain an empirical phenomenon or conceptual statement. The value of a theory increases as the more explanatory power the theory has for the observed phenomenon. What are requirements for developing a new theory on business models? A theoretical contribution in the field of management has to be explicit, consistent, and rich. It should be possible to empirically test the theory and falsify it (Popper, 1982). According to Rynes et al. (2005), a theoretical contribution can inductively construct a new theory, inductively broaden an existing theory, apply a theory in a specific context, initially test a theory, falsify widespread assumptions, or conduct meta-analysis with theoretical implications.

An ideal theory contributes to an existing debate or opens up a new one. In the area of business modelling, a theoretical contribution has to match an empirical phenomenon, for example, the following. What are the antecedents of business models? What are the constitutional elements of a business model? How are business models used in different industries and contexts?

Most of the previous work on business models has tended to build on existing, grand theories, because so-called mainstream science (Kuhn, 1970) is constructed further based on past scientific achievements only. In an ideal traditional world, problems would be solved by universal agreement on the very foundations on which science is based. However, BMI is precisely a radical break from existing dominant logic, and hence, we have decided to approach the research in an analogous way by challenging the conventional manner of research.

The use of different theories is highly encouraged. To support this central argument, Fig. 2.9 roughly approximates which theoretical perspectives are most popular in business innovation and BMI literature. It shows that resource-based theories and knowledge/learning-based theories still form a central foundation in the area.

There are numerous methods for drifting from existing theories (Kuhn, 1970). Empirical insights, experiments, new theories, computation, simulation, as well as data mining support the renewal of existing theories. We want to encourage a broader search for theories explaining business models and BMI in terms of a paradigm shift, in which the existing paradigm of business models and its process of innovation are replaced by a new incompatible paradigm. The challenge lies in the incommensurability of contexts and theoretical contributions. However, this is simultaneously the positive side of the scientific renewal process: we can discover new perspectives and thereby might find new patterns and causal relationships. In this renewal process, business model researchers must be alert to various challenges. Zott and Amit (2013) reflect on five; one of them is the occurring overlap of the idea of business models with other concepts. The authors point out that to avoid confusion, it is essential to carefully distinguish the business model from other existing concepts in literature. Another issue is the critique that the concept lacks independence from other levels of analysis. Zott and Amit (2013) view this circumstance as an opportunity rather than a problem, as it 'points to the need to conduct multilevel research and to integrate theoretical perspectives' (p. 405). Furthermore, business models are sometimes perceived as lacking uniqueness at the level of analysis, and thus, it is crucial to distinctively define the business model to demarcate it from other levels of analysis. This raises the

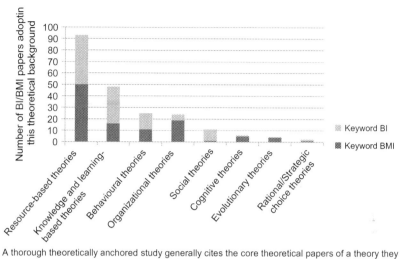

A thorough theoretically anchored study generally cites the core theoretical papers of a theory they are building on (e.g. in the case of the attention-based view, Ocasio (1997)). For each theory, we counted the number of 'theory-citing' papers containing the keywords 'business innovation', and 'business model innovation'. The classification of a specific theory to the respective category is listed in the conclusion (e.g. organizational ambidexterity is categorized in organization theories). The database used is Researchgate, specifically, 'theory-citing papers' considered since 1950.

Fig. 2.9   Theoretical anchoring of studies dealing with business innovation (BI) and business model innovation (BMI) (Note: A thorough theoretically anchored study generally cites the core theoretical papers of a theory they are building on (e.g. in the case of the attention-based view, Ocasio (1997)). For each theory, we counted the number of 'theory-citing' papers containing the keywords 'business innovation', and 'business model innovation'. The classification of a specific theory to the respective category is listed in the conclusion (e.g. organizational ambidexterity is categorized in organization theories). The database used is Researchgate, specifically, 'theory-citing papers' considered since 1950).

challenge of finding 'clean and clear definitions' (Zott & Amit, 2013) to prevent the concept from becoming vague and ambiguous. In addition, solid empirical support to increase the acceptance of the concept is missing. Beyond that, Zott and Amit (2013) plead for more conceptual work to further enhance theoretical development.

The following chapters present existing theories, whose use we want to encourage for the broad area of business modelling. We present a collection of grand theories, although it is far from complete. Nevertheless, it should help researchers consider business models and BMI from different angles. We opt to select a few of the most renowned theories in order to shed more light on the principles and patterns of the business model black box (Chap. 3). We also introduce 30 niche theories in management science (Chap. 4) and suggest applying them to understand what lies behind business models and BMI. By doing so, we hope to enrich the debate on business models, since the field has not yet reached sufficient theoretical depth. We invite management scholars and researchers from various fields to further develop our initial rough suggestions provided herein.[8]

NOTES

1. Main Literature: (Amit & Zott, 2001), (Zott & Amit, 2007, 2008, 2010, 2013), (Amit & Zott, 2015).
2. Main Literature: (Demil & Lecocq, 2010), (Lecocq, Demil, & Ventura, 2010), (Plé, Lecocq, & Angot, 2010).
3. Main literature: (Baden-Fuller & Morgan, 2010), (Baden-Fuller & Haefliger, 2013), (Baden-Fuller & Mangematin, 2013), (Baden-Fuller, 2013).
4. Main literature: (Chesbrough & Rosenbloom, 2002), (Chesbrough, 2006, 2007a, b, 2010), (Teece, 2010), (Leih, Linden, & Teece 2015).
5. Main literature: (Casadesus-Masanell & Ricart, 2010a, 2010b, 2011), (Casadesus-Masanell & Tarziján, 2012), (Casadesus-Masanell & Zhu, 2013).
6. Main literature: (Gassmann, Frankenberger & Csik, 2014), (Frankenberger, Weiblen, Csik & Gassmann, 2013), (Frankenberger, Weiblen, & Gassmann, 2014, 2013).
7. Main literature: (Markides, 1997), (Markides & Charitou, 2004), (Markides, 2006), (Anderson, Markides, & Kupp, 2010), (Markides, 2013), (Markides & Sosa, 2013).
8. Main literature on this section: (Kuhn, 1970), (Reynolds, 1971), (Popper, 1982), (Sutton & Staw, 1995), (Okasha, 2002), (Rynes et al., 2005), (Colquitt & Zapata-Phelan, 2007), (Kriek, Beaty, & Nkomo, 2009), (Jaccard & Jacoby, 2010), (Zott & Amit, 2013).

BIBLIOGRAPHY

Achtenhagen, L., Melin, L., & Naldi, L. (2013). Dynamics of business models–strategizing, critical capabilities and activities for sustained value creation. *Long Range Planning, 46*(6), 427–442.

Afuah, A., & Tucci, C. L. (2001). *Internet Business Models and Strategies*. McGraw-Hill International Editions.

Amit, R., & Zott, C. (2001). Value creation in e-business. *Strategic Management Journal, 22*, 493–520.

Amit, R., & Zott, C. (2015). Crafting business architecture: The antecedents of business model design. *Strategic Entrepreneurship Journal, 9*(4), 331–350.

Anderson, J., Markides, C., & Kupp, M. (2010). The last frontier: Market creation in conflict zones, deep rural areas and urban slums. *California Management Review, 52*(4), 6–28.

Baden-Fuller, C. (2013). What are business models? How the concept can be useful for managers and society. In C. Baden-Fuller (Ed.), *Strategic Management*. London.

Baden-Fuller, C., & Haefliger, S. (2013). Business models and technological innovation. *Long Range Planning, 46*(6), 419–426.

Baden-Fuller, C., & Mangematin, V. (2013). Business models: A challenging agenda. *Strategic Organization, 11*, 418–427.

Baden-Fuller, C., & Morgan, M. S. (2010). Business models as models. *Long Range Planning, 43*(2–3), 156–171.

Baden-Fuller, C., & Winter, S. (2007). *Replicating knowledge practices: Principles or templates*. Working paper, Cass Business School, City University, London.

Casadesus-Masanell, R., & Ricart, J. E. (2010a). From strategy to business models and onto tactics. *Long Range Planning, 43*(2–3), 195–215.

Casadesus-Masanell, R., & Ricart, J. E. (2010b). Competitiveness: Business model reconfiguration for innovation and internationalization. *Management Research: Journal of the Iberoamerican Academy of Management, 8*(2), 123–149.

Casadesus-Masanell, R., & Ricart, J. E. (2011). How to design a winning business model. *Harvard Business Review, 89*(1/2), 100–107.

Casadesus-Masanell, R., & Tarziján, J. (2012, February). When one business model isn't enough. *Harvard Business Review, 90*, 132–137.

Casadesus-Masanell, R., & Zhu, F. (2013). Business model innovation and competitive imitation: The case of sponsor-based business models. *Strategic Management Journal, 34*(4), 464–482.

Cavalcante, S., Kesting, P., & Ulhøi, J. (2011). Business model dynamics and innovation: (Re-) establishing the missing linkages. *Management Decision, 49*(8), 1327–1342.

Chesbrough, H. (2003). The governance and performance of Xerox's technology spin-off companies. *Research Policy, 32*(3), 403–421.

Chesbrough, H. W. (2006). *Open business models: How to thrive in the new innovation landscape*. Boston: Harvard Business Press.

Chesbrough, H. W. (2007a). Business model innovation: It's not just about technology anymore. *Strategy & Leadership, 35*(6), 12–17.

Chesbrough, H. W. (2007b). Why companies should have open business models. *MIT Sloan Management Review, 48*(2), 22.

Chesbrough, H. W. (2010). Business model innovation: Opportunities and barriers. *Long Range Planning, 43*(2–3), 354–363.

Chesbrough, H., & Rosenbloom, R. S. (2002). The role of the business model in capturing value from innovation: Evidence from Xerox Corporation's technology spin-off companies. *Industrial and Corporate Change, 11*(3), 529–555.

Colquitt, J. A., & Zapata-Phelan, C. P. (2007). Trends in theory building and theory testing: A five-decade study of the Academy of Management Journal. *Academy of Management Journal, 50*(6), 1281–1303.

Conley, J. G., Bican, P. M., & Ernst, H. (2013). Value Articulation. *California Management Review, 55*(4), 102–120.

Demil, B., & Lecocq, X. (2010). Business model evolution: In search of dynamic consistency. *Long Range Planning, 43*(2–3), 227–246.

Doganova, L., & Eyquem-Renault, M. (2009). What do business models do? Innovation devices in technology entrepreneurship. *Research Policy, 38*(10), 1559–1570.

Eisenhardt, K. M., & Martin, J. A. (2000). Dynamic capabilities: What are they? *Strategic Management Journal, 21*(10), 1105–1121.

Frankenberger, K., Weiblen, T., Csik, M., & Gassmann, O. (2013a). The 4I-framework of business model innovation: A structured view on process phases and challenges. *International Journal of Product Development, 18*(3), 249–273.

Frankenberger, K., Weiblen, T., & Gassmann, O. (2013b). Network configuration, customer centricity, and performance of open business models: A solution provider perspective. *Industrial Marketing Management, 42*(5), 671–682.

Frankenberger, K., Weiblen, T., & Gassmann, O. (2014). The antecedents of open business models: An exploratory study of incumbent firms. *R&D Management, 44*(2), 173–188.

Gassmann, O., Frankenberger, K., & Csik, M. (2014). *The business model navigator: 55 models that will revolutionise your business.* Harlow: Pearson Education Ltd.

Hamel, G. (2000). *Leading the revolution Harvard Business School Press.* Boston: Harvard Business School Press.

Hargadon, A. B. (2002). *Brokering knowledge: Linking learning and innovation. Research in organizational behavior* (Vol. 24). London: Elsevier.

Hedman, J., & Kalling, T. (2003). The business model concept: Theoretical underpinnings and empirical illustrations. *European Journal of Information Systems, 12*(October 2002), 49–59.

Jaccard, J., & Jacoby, J. (2010). *Theory construction and model-building skills: A practical guide for social scientists.* Guilford Press.

Kriek, H. S., Beaty, D., & Nkomo, S. (2009). Theory building trends in international management research: an archival review of preferred methods: management. *South African Journal of Economic and Management Sciences Suid-Afrikaanse Tydskrif Vir Ekonomiese En Bestuurswetenskappe, 12*(1), 126–135.

Kuhn, T. S. (1970). *The structure of scientific revolutions. Philosophical Review, 2.*

Lakatos, I. (1971). History of science and its rational reconstructions. In R. Buck & R. Cohen (Eds.), *PSA 1970: Proceedings of the 1970 biennial meeting philosophy of science association – In memory of Rudolf Carnap* (Vol. 8, pp. 91–136). Dordrecht: Springer Netherlands.

Lavie, D., Kang, J., & Rosenkopf, L. (2011). Balance Within and Across Domains: The Performance Implications of Exploration and Exploitation in Alliances. *Organization Science, 22*(6), 1517–1538.

Lecocq, X., Demil, B., & Ventura, J. (2010). Business models as a research program in strategic management: An appraisal based on Lakatos. *M@n@gement, 4,* 214–225.

Leih, S., Linden, G., & Teece, D. (2015). Business model innovation and organizational design: A dynamic capabilities perspective. In N. J. Foss & T. Saebi (Eds.), *Business model innovation – The organizational dimension* (pp. 24–42). Oxford: Oxford University Press Inc.

Lieberman, M. B., & Montgomery, D. B. (1988). First-mover advantages. *Strategic management journal, 9*(S1), 41–58.

Magretta, J. (2002). Why business models matter. *Harvard Business Review, 80,* 86–87.

Markides, C. (1997). Strategic innovation. *Sloan Management Review, 38*(3), 9–23.

Markides, C. (2006). Disruptive innovation: In need of better theory. *Journal of Product Innovation Management, 23,* 19–25.

Markides, C. (2013). Business model innovation: What can the ambidexterity literature teach us? *The Academy of Management Perspectives, 27*(4), 313–323.

Markides, C., & Charitou, C. D. (2004). Competing with dual business models: A contingency approach. *Academy of Management Executive, 18*(3), 22–36.

Markides, C., & Sosa, L. (2013). Pioneering and first mover advantages: The importance of business models. *Long Range Planning, 46*(4–5), 325–334.

Martins, L. L., Rindova, V. P., & Greenbaum, B. E. (2015). Unlocking the hidden value of concepts: A cognitive approach to business model innovation. *Strategic Entrepreneurship Journal, 9,* 99–117.

Massa, L., & Tucci, C. L. (2014). Business model innovation. In *The Oxford handbook of innovation management* (pp. 420–441). Oxford: Oxford University Press.

Morris, M., Schindehutte, M., & Allen, J. (2005). The entrepreneur's business model: Toward a unified perspective. *Journal of Business Research, 58,* 726–735.

Malone, T., Weill, P., Lai, R., D'Urso, V., Herman, G., Apel, T., & Woerner, S. (2006). Do Some Business Models Perform Better than Others? *MIT Sloan Research Paper No. 4615–06.*

Ocasio, W. (1997). Towards an Attention Based View of the Firm. *Strategic Management Journal, 18*(S1), 187–206.

Okasha, S. (2002). *Philosophy of science: A very short introduction.* Oxford University Press.

O Reilly, C. A., & Tushman, M. L. (2004). The ambidextrous organization. *Harvard business review, 82*(4), 74-83.

Osterwalder, A., Pigneur, Y., & Clark, T. (2010). *Business model generation : A handbook for visionaries, game changers, and challengers.* Hoboken: Wiley.

Pateli, A. G., & Giaglis, G. M. (2004). A research framework for analysing eBusiness models. *European Journal of Information Systems, 13*(4), 302–314.

Penrose, E. (1960). The growth of the firm—a case study: the Hercules Powder Company. *Business History Review, 34*(1), 1–23.

Plé, L., Lecocq, X., & Angot, J. (2010). Customer-integrated business models: A theoretical framework. *Management, 13*(4), 226–265.

Popper, K. R. (1982). *Logik der Forschung* (Vol. 4.). JCB Mohr (Paul Siebeck)

Porter, M. E. (1985). *Competitive advantage.* New York: Free Press.

Reynolds, P. D. (1971). *A primer in theory construction.* Indianapolis: Bobbs-Merrill Company.

Rynes, S. L., Hillman, A., Ireland, R. D., Kirkman, B., Law, K., Miller, C. C., et al. (2005). Everything you've always wanted to know about AMJ (but may have been afraid to ask). *Academy of Management Journal, 48*(5), 732–737.

Shafer, S. M., Smith, H. J., & Linder, J. C. (2005). The power of business models. *Business Horizons, 48,* 199–207.

Simon, H. A. (1976). *Administrative Behavior. A Study of Decision-Making Processes in Administrative Organization* (Third Edit.). London, UK: The Free Press, Collier Macmillan Publishers.

Sutton, R. I., & Staw, B. M. (1995). What Theory is Not. *Administrative Science Quarterly, 40*(3), 371–384.

Teece, D. J. (2006). Reflections on "profiting from innovation". *Research Policy, 35*(8), 1131–1146.

Teece, D. J. (2010). Business models, business strategy and innovation. *Long Range Planning, 43*(2–3), 172–194.

Teece, D. (2012). Dynamic capabilities: Routines versus entrepreneurial action. *Journal of Management Studies, 49*(8), 1395–1401.

Teece, D., & Pisano, G. (1994). The dynamic capabilities of firms: An introduction. *Industrial and Corporate Change, 3*(3), 537–556.

Teece, D. J., Pisano, G., & Shuen, A. (1997). Dynamic capabilities and strategic management. *Strategic Management Journal, 18*(7), 509–533.

Wirtz, B. W., Pistoia, A., Ullrich, S., & Göttel, V. (2015). Business models: Origin, development and future research perspectives. *Long Range Planning, 49,* 36–54.

Zott, C., & Amit, R. (2007). Business model design and the performance of entrepreneurial firms. *Organization Science, 18*(March 2015), 181–199.

Zott, C., & Amit, R. (2008). The fit between product market strategy and business model: Implications for firm performance. *Strategic Management Journal, 26,* 1–26.

Zott, C., & Amit, R. (2009). The business model as the engine of network-based strategies. In *The network challenge* (pp. 259–275). Upper Saddle River: Wharton School Publishing.

Zott, C., & Amit, R. (2010). Business model design: An activity system perspective. *Long Range Planning, 43*(2–3), 216–226.

Zott, C., & Amit, R. (2013). The business model: A theoretically anchored robust construct for strategic analysis. *Strategic Organization, 11*(4), 403–411.

Zott, C., Amit, R., & Massa, L. (2011). The business model: Recent developments and future research. *Journal of management, 37*(4), 1019–1042.

CHAPTER 3

Exploring the Role of Popular Management Theories for BMI Research

Abstract A theory is nothing more than a new tool to provide explanation of an empirical phenomenon or conceptional statement. Many grand theories could contribute to business model research, and they can spice up business model research by helping to look at the phenomenon from new angles. Twenty renowned theories in management science with potential for future research in exploring the field of business models are presented in this chapter. It introduces each of the theories separately in a compact format. In addition, an analysis of the business model literature that has explicitly drawn on the respective theory is presented. Ultimately, avenues for future research are proposed. In doing so, this study is amongst the first analyses that reviews the literature on business models from a theoretical perspective and, as a result, derives principal gaps in the field.

Keywords Business models • Business model innovation • New theoretical views • Review of 20 management theories • Avenues for future research • Future research directions

3.1 Absorptive Capacity Theory

According to Cohen and Levinthal (2015), *absorptive capacity* is 'the ability of a firm to recognize the value of new, external information, assimilate it, and apply it to commercial ends' (p. 128). Absorptive capacity is critical to firms' innovative capabilities, as it defines the limit of a firm's rate or

47
O. Gassmann et al., *Exploring the Field of Business Model Innovation*,
DOI 10.1007/978-3-319-41144-6_3

quantity of absorption of technological and scientific information. The theory suggests that the absorption of external and new knowledge 'is largely a function of the firm's level of prior related knowledge' (p. 128). Put differently, the more a firm holds or creates internal knowledge (e.g. in R&D), the higher is the probability of innovative performance, as more external knowledge may be absorbed. However, this occurs alongside history- and path dependency.   ·

Zahra and George (2002) propose a conceptualization of absorptive capacities, consisting of the four dimensions of identification, assimilation, transformation, and exploitation of external knowledge. According to Enkel and Mezger (2013), absorptive capacity is in turn operationalized through different learning processes. Exploratory learning enables the acquisition of external knowledge, exploitative learning enables a company to apply the acquired knowledge in a new setting, for example, through combining technological and market knowledge (Lenox & King, 2004; Rothaermel & Deeds, 2004), whereas transformative learning links these two learning processes by maintaining and reactivating acquired knowledge (Lane, Koka, & Pathak, 2006).

Absorptive capacity is crucial as business models are viewed as results of sophisticated strategic decisions whose quality is highly dependent on a broad knowledge base. A well-developed absorptive capacity could, therefore, reduce uncertainties and the number of degrees of freedom in a strategic game. In spite of these enhancements, absorptive capacity might impede BMI. The more knowledge a company gains about its industry, the more difficult it becomes to develop an external, objective perspective on the dominant logic and business model to innovate and gather new insights. In this context, the theory is highly relevant for the development and implementation of business model patterns offered by Gassmann, Frankenberger, and Csik (2014). It involves the absorption of new trends and the increase of learning potential from other industries. Jansen, Bosch, and Volberda (2005) reason that cross-functional and broad interdisciplinary knowledge forms an important basis for absorptive capacity. Cross-industry BMIs may be enabled by absorbing this external knowledge on the basis of abstracting the own model, analogy building with the means of business model patterns, and identifying the right path for the transfer of analogies to the own firm.

Following the work of Zott and Amit (2010), adopting an absorptive capacity theory might help to understand how knowledge about design elements and themes is gathered to improve the business model in different dimensions (e.g. novelty). For Chesbrough and Rosenbloom's (2002) approach, improved absorptive capacity might be another way to circumvent the internal barriers of cognitive limitation and the bias stemming from the existing business model. Casadesus-Masanell and Ricart's (2010) view on business models may be interlinked with absorptive exploration, as learning might enable a company to sense changes in the environment as early as possible to permanently keep the business model up to date.[1]

3.2 Administrative Behaviour Theory

The *theory of administrative behaviour* states that a firm may be solely characterized by its decision-making processes (the individuals' decision-making processes). Subsequently, in order to structure an optimal administrative body, it is indispensable to understand the processes by which people in organizations take decisions. In classic economics, humans behave and make decisions like homo economicus. Therefore, they behave in a perfectly informed and rational way in order to both maximize utility and minimize costs. However, since humans in real life do not truly behave like perfectly calibrated computers, such economists as Herbert Simon (1947) have discarded theories of rational choice. They have pointed out the limits of human rationality in order to explain how organizations make decisions. The theory proposes the *administrative man* with limited rationality, in contrast to Taylor's *economic man*. Such aspects as the tendency to pursue self-interests or that humans are willing to settle for an adequate solution rather than continue seeking an optimal one are also taken into consideration. According to Simon (1990), such limitations have a practical nature and are not static 'but depend upon the organizational environment in which the individuals' decisions take place (...) The task of administration is so to design this environment that the individual will approach as close as practicable to rationality (judged in terms of the organization's goals) in his decisions' (Simon, 1947, p. 240).

This implies that managers might stop innovating their business model once it is *good enough*, yet, BMI projects must be striven for to their maximum potential and pushed even further to achieve success and satisfactory sustainability. Using the theory of administrative behaviour, the irrational behaviour of managers could be more carefully analysed for the implementation of innovative business models. In devising a business model, administrative behaviour theory may help to reveal insights on how to implement an incentive system that fosters a continuous innovation process of the business model by taking rational decision making into account.[2]

3.3   Agency Theory (Principal–Agent Problem)

The principal–agent theory, as one of the prevailing theories in business administration, is embedded within the concept of new institutional economics. The relationship of a principal (e.g. employer) and his agent (e.g. employee) is put into focus, whereupon the basic assumption is incomplete and asymmetric information distribution between the two parties. Considering a common starting point of economic activities, an agent is usually hired by a principal to fulfil a job. A key finding is that the agent typically has a knowledge advantage. Various mechanisms may be used to try to align the interests of the agent with those of the principal, such as piece rates/commissions, profit sharing, efficiency wages, the agent posting a bond, or the fear of being fired. In explaining this complex interdependency, one immediate output of the theory is to help draw conclusions for the drafting of contracts.

Delegation of BMI projects (top down) during implementation often leads to failures. This empirical observation may be explained by agency theory: the failure is due to information asymmetries between decision-making top management and middle management, which has to implement the new business model. A central line of reasoning in this regard is based on the drafting of contracts and the respective incentive systems. Since these managerial systems are generally tailored to the principal–agent problem, they are often directed at exploitation and thus, may impede BMI.[3]

3.4   Behavioural Decision Theory

The quintessence of behavioural decision theory (BDT), similar to the theory of administrative behaviour, is to display how organizations may be comprehended with regard to their decision processes (Simon, 1976). The theory aims to analyse and describe actual decision-making tendencies; once understood, these can be addressed by designing and intervening with appropriate decision support systems. BDT is a descriptive theory of human decision making that builds on rational decision making but includes such assumptions as limited human information-processing capacities and limited willingness to engage in organizations. In contrast to administrative behaviour theory, the approach of BDT is *behavioural* rather than *logical*, as it claims decision-making processes as *human behaviour* for which empirical evidence and determinants have to be identified.

Aspara, Lamberg, Laukia, and Tikkanen (2011) enquire into how cognitive processes and high-echelon/top-management decision processes influence corporate business model transformation decisions. For the case of Nokia, the authors found that selection decisions were influenced by the current reputational rankings of operational businesses and decided by which businesses were retained or divested. Business models that embodied elements which were attributed to past failure were eliminated. In addition, business model researchers could address various other topics, such as decisions that have to be made during the BMI process. Which division should innovate its business model and when should they start with BMI? Moreover, the business model selection process is an under-researched area. BDT could explore issues of limited human information-processing capacities or hesitance to engage in BMI.[4]

3.5   MANAGERIAL COGNITION

There is a broad array of research veins connecting cognition and management research, and the field is determined by an analysis of different constructs. Central themes are *schemata, cognitive maps, dominant logic*, and *boundary objects*, which are described in the following sections.

3.5.1   Schemata

Schemata are active cognitive structures that frame problems (Neisser, 1976, p. 6; Schwenk, 1988). The term *schema* is very much interwoven with the concept of *dominant logic*, as schemas may be understood as frames of reference and interpreted as a means to structure information. In fact, they are considered as means to form mental representations of complex matters. In this way, managers can make use of schemas to categorize and assess events and their consequences, which allows managers to take action rapidly and efficiently. As follows, schemata release managers and organizations of the task of analysing a myriad of uncertain and ambiguous situations (Prahalad & Bettis, 1986). Put differently, schemas 'represent beliefs, theories, and propositions that have developed over time based on the manager's personal experiences' (Prahalad & Bettis, 1986, p. 489). Thus, schemata are previously developed cognitive representations adopted for future problems.[5]

3.5.2   Cognitive Maps

It is not possible to draw a clear line between the concept of schemata and *cognitive maps*. However, it is argued that schema is a broader term, and cognitive maps may be described as 'a particular type of schema or a part of a broader schema' (Weick, 1979, pp. 48–53) and are a way to make sense of a certain phenomenon.

Cognitive maps were first studied in the context of exploring the learning effects of rats and human beings. In this regard, Tolman (1948) argues that cognitive maps are formed by certain concepts, which deal with aspects of the decision environment and cause-and-effect relationships. Thus, such maps help decision makers to classify issues important for diagnosis. Similarly, Eden (1988, p. 262) considers cognitive maps 'as a picture or visual aid in comprehending the mappers' understanding of particular, and selective, elements of the thoughts (rather than thinking) of an individual, group or organization'. On the basis of cognitive maps, people make decisions in the present, derive explanations of the past, or make predictions about the future (Schwenk, 1988).[6]

3.5.3   Dominant Logic

Dominant logic has been a central object of investigation in general management and, especially, among innovation scholars for the past years. It is a term used similarly for schemata and cognitive maps. Generally, dominant logic describes the notion and mental conceptualization of how an industry works and by which means the company has succeeded in the past. It can be described as a mind-set that determines how decisions are made and how goals are achieved. More precisely, dominant logic underlies mental maps, which advance through experience in the core business as well as through sometimes inappropriate application in other fields (Prahalad & Bettis, 1986). Put in a more theoretical frame, 'The dominant logic is stored via schemas and hence can be thought of as a structure. However, some of what is stored is process knowledge' (Prahalad & Bettis, 1986, p. 490). Research is rooted in strategic management and mainly based on competition or diversification. Hence, strategic diversity or multi-unit activities require the management of multiple types of dominant logic. The research group around Prahalad and Bettis has mainly developed the field. However, literature on dominant logic has been extended recently in a seminal article of Vargo and Lusch (2004), who discuss the importance of a *service-dominant logic* for marketing research. Nonetheless, common to all research is the notion that dominant logic is stored as a shared cognitive map (Prahalad & Bettis, 1986).[7]

3.5.4   Boundary Objects

The central research object in this field is the differing usage of information, such as terms or communities (e.g. different business divisions or functions). This is due to the fact that uniform context often becomes contextualized and thereby treated differently by distinct social communities. In such a case, this construct may be termed overarchingly by a single *boundary object*. Put differently, the boundary object must be defined and structured to be common enough for use through several different parties, yet plastic enough and strongly structured to adapt to local needs. To drive relationships between different business divisions, a boundary object is a means to make an object recognizable and translatable to several communities. As such, the creation and management of boundary objects is a key tool in developing and maintaining common comprehension across intersecting departments and functions.[8]

3.5.5   Summary: Business Models and the Cognitive Perspective

Research on cognitive views in management research has received increasing attention (*International Journal of Management Reviews*, Special Issue, April 2015: The Mind in the Middle: Taking Stock of Affect and Cognition Research in Entrepreneurship).

For instance, Martins et al. (2015) state that research on business models has so far focused on a rational positioning or an evolutionary view but mostly neglects the cognitive perspective. According to the authors, this may provide a new opportunity to innovate the business model purposefully instead of solely reacting to exogenous shocks. The field is highly relevant for business model research, and several scholars have started to follow this stream (Baden-Fuller, Mangematin, Doganova, Doz, and Kosonen, see Introduction).

Martins et al. (2015) make use of schemas as a concept to organize knowledge deliberately to innovate a business model. Schemas consist of attributes (*slots*) filled with different values (*fillers*) and relations. They form a mental representation of a complex issue, such as a business model. The authors describe two different methods, namely analogical reasoning and conceptual combination, to support managers who try to deliberately change their business model. Analogical reasoning hereby looks for similarities between business models to infer new ideas and adapt a business model. On the other hand, conceptual combination focuses on differences between business models in order to create 'novel value-enhancing variants' (Martins et al., 2015, p. 112). With their publication, Martins et al. (2015) contribute to business model research by providing a more systematic and methodological approach to BMI, especially in the absence of exogenous change (p. 112). Furthermore, they call on business model scholars to consider cognitive processes. In addition, their research helps to overcome some of the challenges that business model design faces, like '(1) complexity (Baden-Fuller & Morgan, 2010); (2) the need for integrity across design elements and design themes (Casadesus-Masanell & Ricart, 2010) resulting from the systemic structure of business models; and (3) the draw of familiarity and the inertial nature of business models (Chesbrough & Rosenbloom, 2002)' (p. 114).

Rooted in idea generation, Eppler, Hoffmann, and Bresciani (2011) build on a growing body of literature which argues that artefacts (objects, templates, etc.) can enhance innovation performance in teams: 'the template has a significant positive impact on perceived collaboration, thus serving as a joint boundary object that acts as a collaboration catalyst' (p. 1334). In this regard, the cognitive construct of boundary objects is tackled as 'business model templates'. These represent a kind of boundary object and support cross-unit or cross-industry cooperation. However, the scholars emphasize that using boundary objects in firms might have a significant 'negative impact on perceived creativity' (Eppler et al., 2011, p. 1334). Ultimately, boundary object theory could answer further questions, such as the following two. How is the term business model and BMI embedded in different divisions of a company? How do different functions in a BMI project interpret data on new technologies, customer insights, and trends?

3.6   CONTINGENCY THEORY

Fiedler (1964) developed the contingency approach as a branch of behavioural theory. However, there are domains in *contingency theory* that relate to decision making (e.g. Vroom & Yetton, 1973). The theory generally holds that the way a situation is managed or a company is led is always contingent upon a specific case. Since many internal and external factors influence a situation, leadership and/or organizational styles that have proven effective in one particular situation may not be successful when transferred to another.

Applied to innovation management, Tidd (2001) proposes that external contingencies affect the degree, type, organization, and management of innovation, and that a better fit between these factors improves companies' performance. Smith, Binns, and Tushman (2010) assign a critical role to senior leaders in managing complex business models, which are characterized by contradictory tensions (e.g. global franchise firms must act local), and in handling the exploration and exploitation of BMI processes. This involves success factors, such as commitment building, engagement in conflicts, active learning at multiple levels, and dynamic decision making. In addition, Pateli and Giaglis (2004) develop a methodology to generate contingencies for the evolution of a technology-driven firm's business model.[9]

3.7   THEORY OF DYNAMIC CAPABILITIES

The *theory of dynamic capabilities* has been inspired by several lines of thought, such as the RBV (Barney, 1991; Penrose, 1959), organizational routines (Nelson & Winter, 1982), and Porter's (1979) competitive forces. Based on these frameworks, the theory goes further by broaching the issue of selecting, developing, and renewing resources and not merely the resource choice and protection of a competitive advantage.

At its core, the theory may be traced back to Teece and Pisano (1994), who highlight that firms must dynamically respond to fast-paced and competitive environments through internal capabilities. In this, capabilities need to be identified, deployed, and renewed by the firm. Thus, Teece, Pisano, and Shuen (1997, p. 516) define dynamic capabilities as 'the ability to integrate, build, and reconfigure internal and external competencies to address rapidly changing environments'. In line with other scholars in the field, Eisenhardt and Martin (2000, p. 1105) define dynamic capabilities as 'a set of specific and identifiable processes such as product development, strategic decision making, and alliancing'.

Bock et al. (2012) connect BMI with the concept of strategic flexibility and how firms can attain such flexibility. Strategic flexibility is dependent on the organizational structure and dynamic capabilities of a firm. Subsequently, a company has to develop capabilities and structures to facilitate BMI. The core findings of this study regarding dynamic capabilities are: 'decentralized decision-making via delegation is positively associated with strategic flexibility, but consolidating to core functions is not. A creative organizational culture is associated with outcomes of strategic flexibility, while reliance on partners is not. Finally, the relative amount of effort for BMI positively moderates the relationship between reconfiguration and strategic flexibility' (p. 4). In a broader sense, BMI can be seen as a dynamic capability itself as business models are firm boundary-spanning constructs that integrate and further develop internal and external competencies.[10]

3.8   EVOLUTIONISM

Evolutionary theory, as presented by Darwin in 1858, describes and explains the process of development and transformation of organisms and species over time. The theory holds that species undergo random mutations over time, which may or may not be critical characteristics that enable the species to survive. Darwin calls this *natural selection* and *survival of the fittest*. It should be noted that those mutations and new traits are neither deliberate nor intentional. Evolutionary theory has been applied to a wide range of disciplines, for example, to change processes or organizational theory. Nelson and Winter (1982), for instance, have applied evolutionary theory at the firm level with some companies surviving the competitive conditions while others have failed.

Romanelli (1991) recognizes three clusters of research while observing the evolution of organizations. *Organizational genetics* consider the evolution of organizational forms as products of random variations. *Environmental conditioning* emphasizes entrepreneurial action as key evolutionary mechanisms. Finally, the *emergent social system* considers evolution as arising dynamically 'through the cumulative interactions of entrepreneurs and organizations toward the establishment of a new industry system' (Romanelli, 1991, p. 96).

Research in strategic management makes active use of this theory to explain why internal initiatives fail or succeed within the organization. In this, scholars link the theory to network theory to explore how social networks affect the performance and survival of strategic initiatives (Lechner, Frankenberger, & Floyd, 2010). Thus, Darwin's evolutionism could help us to recognize which business models survive on either an organizational or an industrial level and to examine the dynamics of business model evolution. Habtay (2012) argues that evolutionary theory leads to the development of a functioning strategy, technological capabilities, and profit models within established and successful firms. However, when confronted with a disruptive change in the environment, these fixed components can impede an effective response to the changes. In addition, entrepreneurship literature posits that the imitation of business models is a staple for the early and rapid internationalization of new ventures (Dunford, Palmer, & Benveniste, 2010). This in turn can increase the probability of the venture's survival.[11]

3.9 ORGANIZATIONAL AMBIDEXTERITY

In academia, the term *organizational ambidexterity* is better defined as a firm's capability than a theory itself. Ambidextrous organizations are capable of managing the duality of two seemingly opposite poles. In this regard, ambidexterity has been studied in numerous forms, such as centralization versus decentralization. However, the most common notion among scholars is the management of the tension between *exploration* and *exploitation* (Zimmermann, Raisch, & Birkinshaw, 2015). In the spirit of March's (1991) seminal work, the topic of exploration versus exploitation has been extensively studied in organizational theory with an emphasis on innovation (Ahn, Lee, & Lee, 2006; Danneels, 2006; Lee, Delone, & Epinosa, 2006), partnerships in business alliances (Lavie, Stettner, & Tushman, 2010), and business strategy research (Moore, 2005; O'Reilly & Tushman, 2004).

While exploitative initiatives refine existing capabilities, exploratory initiatives discover new capabilities (Burgelman, 2002; Marx, 2004). The idea behind the concept is that firms that engage in exploitive initiatives (e.g. improving their efficiency) and in explorative initiatives (pursuing renewal and innovation-centred activities) behave ambidextrously. There is no agreement among scholars or practitioners if and how it is feasible to pursue both directions.

The *multi-armed bandit problem* in probability theory broaches the issue of the exploration/exploitation conflict and illustrates the problem of a gambler who faces a row of slot machines and who wants to maximize his rewards. The gambler has no knowledge of the outcomes of each machine, and therefore, faces two mutually exclusive decisions: exploration to acquire more information about the outcomes of other machines or exploitation of the currently known machine. Weber (1992) views the multi-armed bandit problem as a question of how single resources should be allocated among alternative projects.

The multi-armed bandit problem and the exploration/exploitation issue perfectly describe the case of BMI, in which managers must decide between exploiting the firm's current market with its current business model and exploring new potential and possibilities through BMI. *Structural separation* as a means to achieve organizational ambidexterity is a frequently presented argument among business model scholars (Markides, 2013). Ambidexterity literature, however, presents two further forms of ambidexterity which have not been covered sufficiently in business model research, namely the *temporal separation of domains* and *contextual ambidexterity* (Khanagha et al., 2014; Lavie et al., 2011; Markides, 2013; Turner et al., 2013; Winterhalter, Zeschky, & Gassmann, 2015). Although the literature on ambidexterity is well established in academia, all four modes of ambidexterity have not yet been studied together sufficiently in the context of BMI (Markides, 2013). Little is known about which of these mechanisms companies apply to implement dual business models and which factors determine the choice of these mechanisms (Winterhalter et al., 2015). Besides a few notable exceptions, the literature has neglected to analyse the business model as a new unit of analysis when analysing ambidextrous firm behaviour. Noteworthy exceptions are Markides (2013), Winterhalter et al. (2015), as well as Zott and Amit (2007), who incorporate the perspectives of exploration/exploitation.[12]

3.10   GENERAL SYSTEMS THEORY

The foundations of *General Systems Theory* go back to the early twentieth century and the biologist Ludwig von Bertalanffy. The theory is applied in several academic domains, and a bandwidth of specific definitions and concepts have evolved over time (e.g. physics, biology, and sociology). Common to all approaches is the investigation of complex entities and the creation of models to describe the same. Systems can generally be described as open, dynamic, and goal-oriented artefacts that interact with their environment and continually evolve. Central to the concept is the holistic analysis of the arrangement, relationship, and structure of the systems' constituent elements (e.g. input and output, system–environment–boundary, process, state, hierarchy of constituent elements, goal directedness, and information flows).

System theoretical approaches have already been used to explain business models, in particular by Zott and Amit (2010). They focus on activity systems, which include the focal firm, and its partners and stakeholders

in the ecosystem, in order to create and capture value (see section on the activity system school in Chap. 2)[13]

3.11 Path Dependency Theory (Historical Institutionalism)

Path dependency explains that the historical track of the institution has inevitable consequences for current and future decisions and occurrences. Thus, it is a self-perpetuating cycle: actions, decisions, and policies of institutions already decide future ones. Historical institutionalism introduces another important concept, which is the critical juncture: path dependency does not necessarily mean that an institution is doomed to fatality and that paths are entirely inevitable. Times of crisis can cause critical junctures, brutally swaying the institution to another path which had been inconceivable or irrelevant until then.

If the self-perpetuating cycle of path dependency explains how a company's previous and current decisions decide future ones, BMI is a deliberate action brought forward by managers to force a critical juncture to break out of the self-perpetuating cycle. In a longitudinal study, Bohnsack, Pinkse, and Kolk (2014) investigate how path dependencies affect the business models of electric vehicle manufacturers, one an incumbent and the other an entrepreneurial new entrant. The study shows how these two types of market actors approach BMI in distinctive ways. A central finding in their study is that once a business model has been established, only exogenous shocks significantly change path dependency.[14]

3.12 Institutional Theory

This theory aims to explain how institutions affect the characteristics of organizational structures in terms of authoritative guidelines. Institutions generally establish rules, norms, or schemas to which the overall social behaviour of an organization is geared. Institutions, therefore, arrange for reliability and stability as mutual interactions become predictable when people act according to organizations' premises. The theory examines how these institutional mechanisms are created and adapted or eventually fall into disuse.

Institutions that are similar to routines, rules, and norms are considered as legitimate within the industry. Therefore, it is difficult for organizations to break out of the given rules and norms within an industry. However, in order to innovate their business models successfully, firms need to enforce conflict and change in the dominant thinking logic. Often, the term 'business model' or 'BMI' itself is not institutionalized within a firm.[15]

3.13   Knowledge-Based View of the Firm

The *knowledge-based view of the firm* (KBV) is often seen as an advancement of the *resource-based view of the firm*. In contrast to the RBV, which identifies knowledge as one resource among others, the KBV defines knowledge as the strategically most important factor featured with several special characteristics. For instance, knowledge is claimed to be the hardest to imitate and the socially most complex resource. A central goal of KBV scholars is to explore how knowledge management leads to competitive advantages for a firm. The theory building and development are driven mainly by Grant (1996a, 1996b) and Spender (1996).

The KBV is a grand theory to explain several aspects of business models. For example, it can help to disclose how firms can escape their dominant logic, how firms should exchange knowledge across different organizational units, and how business model ideas and concepts evolve as a collaborative learning process. Malhotra (2000) emphasizes the need for an updated knowledge-based framework, as new business environments, such as the transition to the internet era, require the adaptation of existing approaches. Subsequently, the first conceptual framework for knowledge management was introduced, aiming to facilitate BMI processes. Denicolai, Ramirez, and Tidd (2014) address the issue of external and internal knowledge sourcing for BMI in a quantitative study. Since there are complementary interplays between internal and external knowledge for value creation, they find a curvilinear relationship (inverted U-shape) between external knowledge-sourcing intensity and firm growth, depending on diverse degrees of knowledge intensity: 'firms with low levels of internal knowledge benefit most from an *optimal* investment in externally generated knowledge. By contrast, knowledge-intensive firms are relatively freer in defining their knowledge sourcing strategy' (Denicolai, Ramirez, & Tidd, 2014, p. 248).[16]

3.14   Organizational Learning Theory

Organizational learning theory forms part of organizational theories. Argyris (1976) emphasizes the aspect of *learning* within decision-making processes. Against this background, the theory discusses feedback loops concerning the reflection of actions with regard to expected versus obtained outcomes. Organizational learning theory further implies the need for a firm to react and interact with its environment in order to stay competitive. Goals and actions must be adapted accordingly, which requires a process of data acquisition, interpretation, and adaptation. It is important to note that knowledge becomes part of an organizational learning process only if that data is communicated, shared, and stored within a company.

BMI can be seen as an organizational learning process whose antecedents and determinants can be analysed. For instance, Moingeon and Lehmann-Ortega (2010) explore double-loop learning which is needed for the creation of a new business model and the difficulties that are encountered when the old and a new business model exist in parallel (p. 266).[17]

3.15   RESOURCE-BASED VIEW OF THE FIRM

The RBV is one of the most popular theories for understanding sources of competitive advantages. It sheds light on the core resources that are pursued by a company and defines them as tangible and intangible assets that are at the disposal of the company (e.g. capabilities, organizational processes, firm attributes, information, knowledge, and capital) (Barney, 1991). According to the RBV, knowledge on rare and valuable resources that are hard to imitate is the key factor for strategy making and long-term competitive advantages.

The RBV is often used to explain success factors of a strategic initiative, such as BMI, in the context of the own resources and competencies of a company. Zott and Amit (2010) critically discuss the theory, and show that resources do not have to exist internally but can be sourced by external partners. Moreover, the aspect of flexibility of resources as a critical success factor for BMI is not sufficiently captured in the RBV. Demil and Lecocq (2010) find that a firm is sustainable only if it can successfully anticipate and react to emerging change. This is captured under the term *dynamic consistency*, implying that while changing the business model, the firm can still maintain its performance level. It gives 'a dynamic vision of strategy' (p. 244), which circumvents the shortcomings of approaches based on sustainable competitive advantage (i.e. there should be no major changes in an operating business model (Demil and Lecocq, 2010, p. 244)) and of hyper-competition theory (i.e. 'competitive advantages can no longer be seen as sustainable due to extreme competition' (Demil & Lecocq, 2010, p. 244)).

The main focus of the RBV lies only in the internal resources possessed by a firm; hence, the view must be extended to relate the concept to business models. For this purpose, the relational view proposed by Dyer and Singh (1998) takes external resources into consideration. Accordingly, spanning a firm's boundaries by, for instance, including external knowledge leads to new sources of enhanced competitive advantage (Dyer & Singh, 1998). Thus, business models might be seen as an evolution of the resource-based and relational view combining the internal and external perspectives while describing the inter-relationships of the components by also modelling the relationship to the customer in a better way.[18]

3.16   Resource Dependency Theory

Companies are highly interdependent on other social organizations and people. Resource dependency theory (RDT) analyses how organizations' systems are linked to their ecosystems in order to comprehend organizations' behaviour. For instance, the theory focuses on how firms are affected by external resources (e.g. raw materials) and how actions or processes concerning the utilization of external resources lead to competitive advantages (e.g. gathering, altering, or exploiting raw material). A company lacking access to resources, for example, would attempt to attain needed resources by building up partnerships. Moreover, the company would on the one hand strive for independence regarding external resources but on the other hand would attempt to increase the dependency of other organizations on its business. RDT introduces a highly relevant concept for companies, as organizational success and power are increasingly dependent on access, control, and efficient utilization of external resources.

Since the business model is a boundary-spanning concept, the RDT is a highly relevant theory for business model research. For instance, the role of power of a focal firm in an ecosystem could be considered by the RDT in order to understand performance implications. Moreover, within an organization, power plays an important role, through which business models pursued are implemented successfully. Sánchez and Ricart (2010) investigate the extent to which an ecosystem in low-income markets influences BMI. The authors differentiate between interactive and isolated business models. In summary, interactive business models create an ecosystem that coevolves with inputs from global and local partners. This not only helps to change the socio-economic context but also creates value, which becomes a source of a more sustainable competitive advantage.[19]

3.17   SOCIAL CAPITAL THEORY

In contrast to the term *human capital*, which focuses on the value of individuals, *social capital theory* examines social relationships among individuals and in communities. It is a theory rooted in sociology that goes back to Pierre Bourdieu, James Coleman, Mark Granovetter, Robert Putnam, and Loury (see main bibliography). In his definition of social capital, Bourdieu distinguishes two elements: first, the social relationship through which individuals can claim access to resources owned by their associates and second, the amount and quality of those resources (Portes, 1998). In Bourdieu's definition, social capital is conceptualized on the individual level and 'just as physical capital and human capital facilitate productive activity, social capital does as well' (Coleman, 1988, p. 101). Competitive advantages (psychological, emotional, or economic) are generated by establishing these social relationships purposefully.

Social capital can help to explain how the relational capabilities of individuals or groups might influence business model relevant knowledge that has been transferred between organizational units or between organizations.[20]

3.18   SOCIAL NETWORK THEORY

In contrast to traditional sociological studies, *social network theory* emphasizes the analysis of relationships/ties between actors rather than the attributes of individual units/actors. Social network theory defines individual actors as nodes while the relationships between them are represented by ties. Granovetter (1973) contributes to social network theory by introducing the concept of weak and strong ties. Empirical findings in this field show that individual units (e.g. humans) foster strong ties (relationships) to only a limited number of other actors. Consequently, and particularly for economic relationships, weak ties become important as they build bridges to other small network groups and thereby enable an exchange of information between several strong networks. A wide range of methods for analysing the structure of social entities exists in academia.

Social network theory could help to explain how different functions within an organization interact in order to design and successfully implement cross-functional BMI. In addition, it could explain how a network between the focal firm and external partners should be configured in order to increase the probability of success of BMI initiatives. Core constructs for investigation could be tie strength, structural holes, network size and density, as well as cognitive closeness of the partnering firms.[21]

3.19   STAKEHOLDER THEORY

Stakeholder theory is an upcoming tool in management research. Donaldson and Preston (1995) argue that stakeholder theory 'has been advanced and justified in the management literature on the basis of its descriptive accuracy, instrumental power and normative validity' (p. 65). The theory focuses on the analysis of the wide range of parties involved in economic value-creation processes, including customers, employees, investors, suppliers, or communities, such as political groups or trade associations. According to Freeman (2014), two groups of stakeholders can be distinguished. The *narrow definition* includes those groups which are vital to the survival and success of the corporation. The *wide definition* includes any group or individual who can affect or is affected by the corporation. Stakeholder analysts further argue 'that all persons or groups with legitimate interests in participating in an enterprise do so to obtain benefits and that there is no prima facie priority of one set of interests or benefits over another' (Donaldson & Preston, 1995, p. 68). Mitchell, Agle, and Wood (1997), however, argue that stakeholder groups may be categorized according to three attributes: *legitimacy* of a claim on the firm, *power* to influence firm behaviour, and *urgency* of the degree to which stakeholders attract the immediate attention of the company. With their work, the authors aim to provide management with a tool to sort and prioritize their stakeholders in order to set the right focus in their stakeholder management efforts.

Harrison, Bosse, and Philips (2010) posit that a firm, which not only wants to retain the wilful participation of its stakeholders but also tries to satisfy their needs and demands, will use additional resources to manage those stakeholders. Consequently, those firms will receive more detailed information regarding the utility functions of their stakeholders. By managing stakeholders actively and hence, allocating resources to areas that are satisfying, Harrison et al. (2010) theorize that the competitive advantage and degree of innovation of a company increases.

A stakeholder perspective on business models could help us to understand the interplay among partners and the effect of the different interests of the involved actors in the ecosystem. Stakeholder theory is increasingly important in business model research due to the fact that business models by definition span boundaries and include external partners in the value-creation process. Gnatzy and Moser (2012) study the political, economic, socio-cultural, and technological stakeholder approach to show how stakeholder theory could be used for developments of business models, taking as an example the health insurance market in rural India. The key question to ask here is how can firms integrate and work with stakeholders to improve business model performance. Hall and Wagner (2012) find a positive association of the integration of strategic and environmental issues with the economic and environmental performance of firms. In addition, secondary stakeholders influence the sustainability of the implementation of BMIs. Another attempt to combine stakeholder theory and business models is undertaken by Miller, McAdam, and McAdam (2014), who analyse the change process of universities' business models. The changes in content, structure, and governance are the results of different stakeholder stages (i.e. academics, industry liaison staff, technology transfer office staff, and government support agency representatives (p. 265)). Therefore, BMIs are not considered as a process of cocreation but as *a series of transitions.*

Furthermore, stakeholder theory may be applied to internal processes. The enforcement of radically new BMIs in firms involves thorough management of internal stakeholders to push through the idea. Which stakeholders and by what means these stakeholders should be managed to achieve success is an important aspect of business model research, both practically and theoretically.[22]

3.20   Transaction Cost Theory

Transaction cost theory forms part of the new institutional economics. It relates to the overarching concept by arguing that institutions reduce transaction costs as they build a stable structure and reduce uncertainty. According to Williamson (1979), transaction costs are a central topic of economic studies. If they were insignificant, 'any advantages one mode of organization appears to hold over another will simply be eliminated by costless contracting' (p. 233). Transaction costs are defined as costs that occur during economic exchanges and can be categorized into (1) search and information costs, (2) bargaining costs, as well as (3) policing and enforcement costs. Considering transaction costs, a company finds itself in the extremes of either choosing hierarchies (in-house production) or markets as a governance structure.

Transaction cost theory plays an important role in the selection of the business model partners. Specificity of new business models can be analysed by a transaction cost perspective. In all market relevant business models, the existence or design of information asymmetry, which is a crucial part in transaction cost economics, has a strong effect on the bargaining power and asymmetry of the ecosystem as a whole. Business models should thence create value by structuring new sources of efficiency.[23]

NOTES

1. Main Literature: (Cohen & Levinthal, 1990), (Henderson & Cockburn, 1994), (Lane & Lubatkin, 1998), (Van den Bosch, Volberda & de Boer, 1999), (Zahra & George, 2002), (Jansen, Van Den Bosch, & Volberda, 2005), (Lane, Koka, & Pathak, 2006), (Enkel & Mezger, 2013), (Cohen & Levinthal, 2015).
2. *Main Literature*: (Simon, 1947, 1955), (March & Simon, 1958), (Williamson, 1981), (Simon, 1990, 1991), (March, 1994), (Kahneman, 2003).
3. Main Literature: (Alchian & Demsetz, 1972), (Jensen & Meckling, 1976), (Eisenhardt, 1985).
4. Main Literature: (Simon, 1955, 1959), (Cyert & March, 1963), (Todd & Benbasat, 1994).
5. Key Literature: (Neisser, 1976), (Prahalad & Bettis, 1986), (Schwenk, 1988), (Taylor & Crocker, 1983).
6. Key Literature: (Tolman, 1948), (Axelrod, 1976), (Weick, 1979), (Schwenk, 1988), (Eden, 1992), (Fiol & Huff, 1992).
7. Key Literature: (Prahalad & Bettis, 1986), (Grant, 1988), (Bettis & Prahalad, 1995), (Vargo & Lusch, 2004).
8. Main Literature: (Star & Griesemer, 1989), (Bowker & Star, 2000), (Levina & Vaaste, 2004).
9. Main Literature: (Fiedler, 1964), (Lawrence & Lorsch, 1967a, 1967b), (Kast & Rosenzweig, 1972, 1973), (Vroom & Yetton, 1973), (Otley, 1980), (Pateli & Giaglis, 2005).
10. Main Literature: (Helfat, 1997), (Teece, Pisano, & Shuen, 1997), (Eisenhardt & Martin, 2000), (Makadok, 2001), (Winter, 2003).
11. Main Literature: (Nelson & Winter, 1982), (Hannan & Freeman, 1977), (Romanelli, 1991), (Chakravarthy & Doz, 1992), (Gould, 2002).
12. Main Literature: (Weber, 1992), (Gibson & Birkinshaw, 2004), (Raisch et al., 2009), (O'Reilly & Tushman, 2013), (Raisch, Birkinshaw, & Zimmermann, 2015).
13. Main Literature: (Boulding, 1956), (Simon, 1962), (Von Bertalanffy, 1972), (Kast & Rosenzweig, 1972).
14. Main Literature: (Arthur, 1994), (Ruttan, 1997), (Pierson, 2000), (Collier & Collier, 2002), (Sydow, Schreyog, & Koch, 2009).
15. Main Literature: (DiMaggio & Powell, 1983), (Scott, 1987), (Oliver, 1991).
16. Main Literature: (Conner, 1991), (Kogut & Zander, 1992), (Nonaka & Takeuchi, 1995), (Grant, 1996a, 1996b), (Spender, 1996), (Kogut, 2000).
17. Main Literature: (Cyert & March, 1963), (Cangelosi & Dill, 1965), (Argyris, 1967, 1976), (Duncan, 1979), (Daft & Weick, 1984), (Fiol & Lyles, 1985).
18. Main Literature: (Penrose, 1959), (Wernerfelt, 1984), (Barney, 1986a, 1986b,1986c, 1988, 1991), (Mahoney & Pandian, 1992), (Dyer & Singh, 1998).
19. Main Literature: (Pfeffer & Salancik, 1979), (Ulrich & Barney, 1984), (Medcof, 2001), (Tillquist, King, & Woo, 2002).
20. Main Literature: (Granovetter, 1973), (Bourdieu, 1983), (Coleman, 1988), (Putnam, 1993), (Nahapiet & Ghoshal, 1998), (Portes, 1998).

21. Main Literature: (Barnes, 1954), (Granovetter, 1973), (Freeman, 1978), (Ibarra & Andrews, 1993), (Watts & Strogatz, 1998), (Moody & White, 2003), (Burt, 2009).

22. Main Literature: (Freeman, 1984), (Hill & Jones, 1992), (Donaldson & Preston, 1995), (Mitchell, Agle, & Wood, 1997), (Frooman, 1999), (Jones & Wicks, 1999), (Jawahar & McLaughlin, 2001), (Harrison, Bosse, & Philips, 2010), (Freeman, 2014),

23. Main Literature: (Coase, 1937, 1960), (Williamson, 1975), (Klein, Crawford, & Alchian, 1978), (Williamson, 1979, 1981, 1985).

BIBLIOGRAPHY

Ahn, J., Lee, D., & Lee, S. (2006). Balancing business performance and knowledge performance of new product development: Lessons from ITS industry. *Long Range Planning, 39*, 525–542.

Alchian, A. A., & Demsetz, H. (1972). Production, information costs, and economic organization. *The American Economic Review, 62*(5), 777–795.

Argyris, C. (1967). Today's problems with tomorrow's organizations. *Journal of Management Studies, 4*(1), 31–55.

Argyris, C. (1976). Single-loop and double-loop models in research on decision making. *Administrative Science Quarterly, 21*(3), 363–375.

Arthur, W. B. (1994). *Increasing returns and path dependence in the economy.* Michigan: University of Michigan Press.

Aspara, J., Lamberg, J.-A., Laukia, A., & Tikkanen, H. (2011). Strategic management of business model transformation: Lessons from Nokia. *Management Decision, 49*(4), 622–647.

Axelrod, R. (1976). *The structure of decision: Cognitive maps of political elites.* Princeton: Princeton University Press.

Baden-Fuller, C., & Morgan, M. S. (2010). Business models as models. *Long Range Planning, 43*(2–3), 156–171.

Barnes, J. A. (1954). Class and committees in a Norwegian island parish. *Human Relations, 7*(1), 39–58.

Barney, J. B. (1986a). Organizational culture: Can it be a source of sustained competitive advantage ? *The Academy of Management Review, 11*(3), 656–665.

Barney, J. B. (1986b). Strategic factor markets: Expectations, luck, and business strategy. *Management Science, 32*(10), 1231–1241.

Barney, J. B. (1986c). Types of competition and the theory of strategy: Toward an integrative framework. *Academy of Management Review, 11*(4), 791–800.

Barney, J. B. (1988). Returns to bidding firms in mergers and acquisitions: Reconsidering the relatedness hypothesis. *Strategic Management Journal, 9*(S1), 71–78.

Barney, J. B. (1991). Firm resources and sustained competitive advantage. *Journal of Management, 17*, 99–120.

Bettis, R. A., & Prahalad, C. K. (1995). The dominant logic: Retrospective and extension. *Strategic Management Journal, 16*(1), 5–14.

Bock, A. J., Opsahl, T., George, G., & Gann, D. M. (2012). The effects of culture and structure on strategic flexibility during business model innovation. *Journal of Management Studies, 49*(2), 279–305.

Bohnsack, R., Pinkse, J., & Kolk, A. (2014). Business models for sustainable technologies: Exploring business model evolution in the case of electric vehicles. *Research Policy, 43*(2), 284–300.

Boulding, K. E. (1956). General systems theory-the skeleton of science. *Management Science, 2*(3), 197–208.

Bourdieu, P. (1983). Ökonomisches Kapital, kulturelles Kapital, soziales Kapital. In R. Kreckel (Ed.), *Soziale Ungleichheiten* (pp. 183–198). Göttingen: Springer.

Bourdieu, P. (1986). The forms of capital. In *Handbook of theory and research of for the sociology of education* (pp. 241–258). New York: Greenwood Press.

Bowker, G. C., & Star, S. L. (2000). *Sorting things out: Classification and its consequences*. MIT press.

Burgelman, R. A. (2002). Strategy as vector and the inertia of coevolutionary lock-in. *Administrative Science Quarterly, 47*, 325–357.

Burt, R. S. (2009). *Structural holes: The social structure of competition*. Cambridge, MA: Harvard University Press.

Cangelosi, V. E., & Dill, W. R. (1965). Organizational learning : Observations toward a theory. *Administrative Science Quarterly, 10*(2), 175–203.

Casadesus-Masanell, R., & Ricart, J. E. (2010). From strategy to business models and onto tactics. *Long Range Planning, 43*(2–3), 195–215.

Chakravarthy, B. S., & Doz, Y. (1992). Strategy process research: Focusing on corporate self-renewal. *Strategic Management Journal, 13*(S1), 5–14.

Chesbrough, H., & Rosenbloom, R. S. (2002). The role of the business model in capturing value from innovation: Evidence from Xerox Corporation's technology spin-off companies. *Industrial and Corporate Change, 11*(3), 529–555.

Coase, R. H. (1937). The nature of the firm. *Economica, 4*(16), 386–405.

Coase, R. H. (1960). The problem of social cost. *Journal of Law and Economics, 3*(1), 414–440.

Cohen, W. M., & Levinthal, D. A. (1990). Absorptive capacity : A new perspective on learning and innovation. *Administrative Science Quarterly, 35*(1), 128–152.

Cohen, W. M., & Levinthal, D. A. (2015). *Absorptive capacity : A new perspective on and innovation learning, 35*(1), 128–152.

Coleman, J. S. (1988). Social capital in the creation of human capital. *American Journal of Sociology, 94*(S1), S95–S120.

Collier, R. B., & Collier, D. (2002). *Shaping the political arena*. Notre Dame: University of Notre Dame Press.

Conner, K. R. (1991). A historical comparison of resource-based theory and five schools of thought within industrial organization economics: Do we have a new theory of the firm? *Journal of Management, 17*(1), 121–154.

Cyert, R. M., & March, J. G. (1963). *A behavioral theory of the firm*. Englewood Cliffs: Prentice Hall.

Daft, R. L., & Weick, K. E. (1984). Toward a model of organizations as interpretation systems. *Academy of Management Review, 9*(2), 284–295.

Danneels, E. (2006). *Dialogue on the effects of disruptive technology on firms and industries*. Oxford: Blackwell.

Demil, B., & Lecocq, X. (2010). Business model evolution: In search of dynamic consistency. *Long Range Planning, 43*(2–3), 227–246.

Van den Bosch, F. A. J., Volberda, H. W., & de Boer, M. (1999). Coevolution of firm absorptive capacity and knowledge environment: Organizational forms and combinative capabilities. *Organization Science, 10*(5), 551–568.

Denicolai, S., Ramirez, M., & Tidd, J. (2014). Creating and capturing value from external knowledge: The moderating role of knowledge intensity. *R&D Management, 44*(3), 248–264.

DiMaggio, P. J., & Powell, W. W. (1983). The iron cage revisited: Institutional isomorphism and collective rationality in organizational fields. *American Sociological Review, 48*(2), 147–160.

Donaldson, T., & Preston, L. E. (1995). The stakeholder theory of the corporation: Concepts, evidence, and implications. *Academy of Management Review, 20*(1), 65–91.

Duncan, R. (1979). Organizational learning: Implications for organizational design. *Research in Organizational Behavior, 1*, 75–123.

Dunford, R., Palmer, I., & Benveniste, J. (2010). Business model replication for early and rapid internationalisation: The ING direct experience. *Long Range Planning, 43*(5), 655–674.

Dyer, J. H., & Singh, H. (1998). The relational view: Cooperative strategy and sources of interorganizational competitive advantage. *Academy of Management Review, 23*(4), 660–679.

Eden, C. (1988). Cognitive mapping. *European Journal of Operational Research, 36*(1), 1–13.

Eden, C. (1992). On the nature of cognitive maps. *Journal of Management studies, 29*(3), 261–265.

Eisenhardt, K. M. (1985). Control: Organizational and economic approaches. *Management Science, 31*(2), 134–149.

Eisenhardt, M. (1989). Agency theory: An assessment and review. *The Academy of Management Review, 14*(1), 57–74.

Eisenhardt, K. M., & Martin, J. A. (2000). Dynamic capabilities: What are they? *Strategic Management Journal, 21*(10), 1105–1121.

Enkel, E., & Mezger, F. (2013). Imitation processes and their application for business model innovation: An explorative study. *International Journal of Innovation Management, 17*(01).

Eppler, M. J., Hoffmann, F., & Bresciani, S. (2011). New business models through collaborative idea generation. *International Journal of Innovation Management, 15*(06), 1323–1341.

Fiedler, F. E. (1964). A contingency model of leadership effectiveness. *Advances in Experimental Social Psychology, 1(1)*, 149–190.

Fiol, C. M., & Huff, A. S. (1992). Maps for managers: Where are we? Where do we go from here? *Journal of Management Studies, 29(3)*, 267–285.

Fiol, C. M., & Lyles, M. A. (1985). Organizational learning. *The Academy of Management Review, 10(4)*, 803–813.

Freeman, L. C. (1978). Centrality in social networks conceptual clarification. *Social Networks, 1(3)*, 215–239.

Freeman, R. E. (1984). *Strategic management : A stakeholder approach*. Marshfield: Pitman Publishing.

Freeman, R. E. (2014). Stakeholder theory of the modern corporation. In W. M. Hoffman, R. E. Frederick, & M. S. Schwartz (Eds.), *Business ethics: Readings and cases in corporate morality* (pp. 184–191). New York: Wiley.

Frooman, J. (1999). Stakeholder influence strategies. *The Academy of Management Review, 24(2)*, 191–205.

Gassmann, O., Frankenberger, K., & Csik, M. (2014). *The business model navigator: 55 models that will revolutionise your business*. Harlow: Pearson Education Ltd..

Gibson, C. B., & Birkinshaw, J. (2004). The antecedents, consequences, and mediating role of organizational ambidexterity. *Academy of Management Journal, 47(2)*, 209–226.

Gnatzy, T., & Moser, R. (2012). Scenario development for an evolving health insurance industry in rural India: INPUT for business model innovation. *Technological Forecasting and Social Change, 79(4)*, 688–699.

Gould, S. J. (2002). *The structure of evolutionary theory*. Cambridge, MA: Harvard University Press.

Granovetter, M. S. (1973). The strength of weak ties. *The American Journal of Sociology, 78(6)*, 1360–1380.

Granovetter, M. S. (1983). The strength of weak ties: A network theory revisited. *Sociological Theory, 1(1983)*, 201–233.

Grant, R. M. (1988). On 'dominant logic', relatedness and the link between diversity and performance. *Strategic Management Journal, 9(6)*, 639–642.

Grant, R. M. (1996a). Prospering in dynamically-competitive environments: Organizational capability as knowledge integration. *Organization Science, 7(4)*, 375–387.

Grant, R. M. (1996b). Toward a knowledge-based theory of the firm. *Strategic Management Journal, 17(S2)*, 109–122.

Habtay, S. R. (2012). A firm-level analysis on the relative difference between technology-driven and market-driven disruptive business model innovations. *Creativity and Innovation Management, 21(3)*, 290–303.

Hall, J., & Wagner, M. (2012). Integrating sustainability into firms' processes: Performance effects and the moderating role of business models and innovation. *Business Strategy and the Environment, 21(3)*, 183–196.

Hannan, M. T., & Freeman, J. (1977). The population ecology of organizations. *American Journal of Sociology, 82*(5), 929–964.

Harrison, J. S., Bosse, D. A., & Phillips, R. A. (2010). Managing for stakeholders, stakeholder utility functions, and competitive advantage. *Strategic Management Journal, 31*(1), 58–74.

Helfat, C. E. (1997). Know-how and asset complementarity and dynamic capability accumulation. *Strategic Management Journal, 18*(5), 339–360.

Henderson, R., & Cockburn, I. (1994). Measuring competence? Exploring firm effects in pharmaceutical research. *Strategic Management Journal, 15*(Winter), 63–84.

Hill, C. W. L., & Jones, T. M. (1992). Stakeholder-agency theory. *Journal of Management Studies, 29*(2), 131–154.

Ibarra, H., & Andrews, S. B. (1993). Power, social influence, and sense making: Effects of network centrality and proximity on employee perceptions. *Administrative Science Quarterly, 38*(2), 277–303.

Jansen, J. J. P., Van Den Bosch, F. A. J., & Volberda, H. W. (2005). Managing potential and realized absorptive capacity: How do organizational antecedents matter? *The Academy of Management Journal, 48*(6), 999–1015.

Jawahar, I., & McLaughlin, G. (2001). Toward a descriptive stakeholder theory: An organizational life cycle approach. *Academy of Management Review, 26*(3), 397–414.

Jensen, M. C., & Meckling, W. H. (1976). Theory of the firm: Managerial behavior, agency costs, and ownership structure. *Journal of Financial Economics, 3*(4), 305–360.

Jones, T. M., & Wicks, A. C. (1999). Convergent stakeholder theory. *Academy of Management Review, 24*(2), 206–221.

Kahneman, D. (2003). Maps of bounded rationality: Psychology for behavioral economics. *The American Economic Review, 93*(5), 1449–1475.

Kast, F. E., & Rosenzweig, J. E. (1972). General systems theory: Applications for organization and management. *Academy of management journal, 15*(4), 447–465.

Kast, F. E., & Rosenzweig, J. E. (1973). *Contingency views of organization and management.* Chicago: Science Research Associates.

Khanagha, S., Volberda, H., & Oshri, I. (2014). Business model renewal and ambidexterity : Structural alteration and strategy formation process during transition to a Cloud business model. *R&D Management, 44*(3), 322–340.

Klein, B., Crawford, R. G., & Alchian, A. A. (1978). Vertical integration, appropriable rents, and the competitive contracting process. *The Journal of Law and Economics, 21*(2), 297–326.

Kogut, B. (2000). The network as knowledge: Generative rules and the emergence of structure. *Strategic Management Journal, 21*(3), 405–425.

Kogut, B., & Zander, U. (1992). Knowledge of the firm, combinative capabilities, and the replication of technology. *Organization Science, 3*(3), 383–397.

Lane, P. J., & Lubatkin, M. (1998). Relative absorptive capacity and interorganization learning. *Strategic Management Journal, 19*(5), 461–477.

Lane, P. J., Koka, B. R., & Pathak, S. (2006). The reification of absorptive capacity: A critical review of the construct. *Academy of Management Review, 31*(4), 833–863.

Lavie, D., Kang, J., & Rosenkopf, L. (2011). Balance Within and Across Domains: The Performance Implications of Exploration and Exploitation in Alliances. *Organization Science, 22*(6), 1517–1538.

Lavie, D., Stettner, U., & Tushman, M. L. (2010). Exploration and exploitation within and across organizations. *The Academy of Management Annals, 4*(1), 109–155.

Lawrence, P. R., & Lorsch, J. W. (1967a). *Organization and environment.* Cambridge, MA: Harvard University Press.

Lawrence, P. R., & Lorsch, J. W. (1967b). Differentiation and integration in complex organizations. *Administrative science quarterly,* 1–47.

Lechner, C., Frankenberger, K., & Floyd, S. W. (2010). Task contingencies in the curvilinear relationships between intergroup networks and initiative performance. *Academy of Management Journal, 53*(4), 865–889.

Lee, G., Delone, W., & Epinosa, J. A. (2006). Ambidextrous coping strategies in globally distributed software development projects. *Communications of the ACM, 49,* 35–40.

Lenox, M. J., & King, A. (2004). Prospects for developing absorptive capacity through internal information provision. *Strategic Management Journal, 25*(4), 331–345.

Levina, N., & Vaaste, E. (2004). The emergence of boundary spanning competence in practice: Implications for information systems' implementation use. Information systems working papers series, New York University, Stern School of Business & Long Island University.

Mahoney, J. T., & Pandian, J. R. (1992). The resource-based view within the conversation of strategic management. *Strategic Management Journal, 13*(5), 363–380.

Makadok, R. (2001). Toward a synthesis of the resource-based and dynamic-capability views of rent creation. *Strategic Management Journal, 22*(5), 387–401.

Malhotra, Y. (Ed.) (2000). *Knowledge management and virtual organizations.* Hershey: IGI Global.

March, J. G. (1991). Exploration and exploitation in organizational learning. *Organization Science, 2,* 71–87.

March, J. G. (1994). *Primer on decision making: How decisions happen.* Simon and Schuster.

March, J. G., & Simon, H. A. (1958). *Organizations.* New York: Wiley.

Markides, C. (2013). Business model innovation: What can the ambidexterity literature teach us? *The Academy of Management Perspectives, 27*(4), 313–323.

Martins, L. L., Rindova, V. P., & Greenbaum, B. E. (2015). Unlocking the hidden value of concepts: A cognitive approach to business model innovation. *Strategic Entrepreneurship Journal, 9*, 99–117.

Marx, K. (2004). *The role of the social context for strategy-making : Examining the impact of embeddedness on the performance of strategic initiatives.* Wiesbaden: Deutscher Universitätsverlag.

Medcof, J. W. (2001). Resource-based strategy and managerial power in networks of internationally dispersed technology units. *Strategic Management Journal, 22*(11), 999–1012.

Miller, K., McAdam, M., & McAdam, R. (2014). The changing university business model: A stakeholder perspective. *R&D Management, 44*(3), 265–287.

Mitchell, R. K., Agle, B. R., & Wood, D. J. (1997). Toward a theory of stakeholder identification and salience : Defining the principle of who and what really counts. *Academy of Management Review, 22*(4), 853–886.

Moingeon, B., & Lehmann-ortega, L. (2010). Creation and implementation of a new business model : A disarming case study. *Management, 13*(4), 266–297.

Moody, J., & White, D. R. (2003). Structural cohesion and embeddedness: A hierarchical concept of social groups. *American Sociological Review, 68*(1), 103–127.

Moore, G. A. (2005). Strategy and your stronger hand (cover story). *Harvard Bsiness Review, 83*, 62–72.

Nahapiet, J., & Ghoshal, S. (1998). Social capital, intellectual capital, and the organizational advantage. *The Academy of Management Review, 23*(2), 242–266.

Neisser, U. (1976). *Cognition and reality.* San Francisco: Freeman.

Nelson, R. R., & Winter, S. G. (1982). *An evolutionary theory of economic change.* Belknap: Cambridge, MA.

Nonaka, I., & Takeuchi, H. (1995). *The knowledge-creating company: How Japanese companies create the dynamics of innovation.* Oxford: Oxford University Press.

O Reilly, C. A., & Tushman, M. L. (2004). The ambidextrous organization. *Harvard business review, 82*(4), 74-83

O'Reilly, C., & Tushman, M. L. (2013). Organizational ambidexterity: Past, present and future. *Academy of Management Perspectives, 27*(4), 324–338.

Oliver, C. (1991). Strategic responses to institutional processes. *Academy of Management Review, 16*(1), 145–179.

Otley, D. T. (1980). The contingency theory of management accounting: Achievement and prognosis. *Accounting, Organizations and Society, 5*(4), 413–428.

Pateli, A. G., & Giaglis, G. M. (2004). A research framework for analysing eBusiness models. *European Journal of Information Systems, 13*(4), 302–314.

Pateli, A. G., & Giaglis, G. M. (2005). Technology innovation-induced business model change: A contingency approach. *Journal of Organizational Change Management, 18*(2), 167–183.

Penrose, E. T. (1959). *The theory of the growth of the firm*. New York: Wiley.

Pfeffer, J., & Salancik, G. (1979). *The external control of organizations: A resource dependence perspective*. New York: Harper & Row.

Pierson, P. (2000). Increasing returns, path dependence, and the study of politics. *American Political Science Review, 94*(02), 251–267.

Porter, M. (1979). How competitive forces shape strategy. *Harvard Buesiness Review*, 137–145.

Portes, A. (1998). Social capital: Its origins and applications in modern sociology. *Annual Review of Sociology, 24*(1), 1–24.

Prahalad, C. K., & Bettis, R. A. (1986). The dominant logic: A new linkage between diversity and performance. *Strategic Management Journal, 7*(6), 485–501.

Putnam, R. D. (1993). The prosperous community: Social capital and economic growth. *The American Prospect, 4*(13), 35–42.

Raisch, S., Birkinshaw, J., Probst, G., & Tushman, M. L. (2009). Organizational ambidexterity: Balancing exploitation and exploration for sustained performance. *Organization Science, 20*(4), 685–695.

Raisch, S., Birkinshaw, J., & Zimmermann, A. (2015). How is ambidexterity initiated? The emergent charter definition process. *Organization Science, 26*(2), 1–21.

Romanelli, E. (1991). The evolution of new organizational forms. *Annual Review of Sociology, 17*, 79–103.

Rothaermel, F. T., & Deeds, D. L. (2004). Exploration and exploitation alliances in biotechnology: A system of new product development. *Strategic Management Journal, 25*(3), 201–221.

Ruttan, V. W. (1997). Induced innovation, evolutionary theory and path dependence: Sources of technical change. *The Economic Journal, 107*(444), 1520–1529.

Sánchez, P., & Ricart, J. E. (2010). Business model innovation and sources of value creation in low-income markets. *European Management Review, 7*(3), 138–154.

Schwenk, C. R. (1988). The cognitive perspective on strategic decision making. *Journal of Management Studies, 25*(1), 41–55.

Scott, W. R. (1987). The adolescence of institutional theory. *Administrative Science Quarterly, 32*(4), 493–511.

Simon, H. A. (1947). *Administrative behavior; A study of decision-making processes in administrative organization*. New York: Macmillan.

Simon, H. A. (1955). A behavioral model of rational choice. *The Quarterly Journal of Economics, 69*(1), 99–118.

Simon, H. A. (1959). Theories of decision-making in economics and behavioral science. *The American Economic Review, 49*(3), 253–283.

Simon, H. A. (1962). The architecture of complexity. *Proceedings of the American Philosophical Society, 106*, 467–482.

Simon, H. A. (1976). *Administrative Behavior. A Study of Decision-Making Processes in Administrative Organization* (Third Edit.). London, UK: The Free Press, Collier Macmillan Publishers.

Simon, H. A. (1990). A mechanism for social selection and successful altruism. *Science, 250*(4988), 1665–1668.

Simon, H. A. (1991). Organizations and markets. *The Journal of Economic Perspectives, 5*(2), 25–44.

Smith, W. K., Binns, A., & Tushman, M. L. (2010). Complex business models: Managing strategic paradoxes simultaneously. *Long Range Planning, 43*(2-3), 448–461.

Spender, J. C. (1996). Making knowledge the basis of a dynamic theory of the firm. *Strategic Management Journal, 17*(S2), 45–62.

Star, S. L., & Griesemer, J. R. (1989). Institutional ecology, 'translations' and boundary objects: Amateurs and professionals in Berkeley's museum of vertebrate zoology, 1907–39. *Social Studies of Science, 19*(3), 387–420.

Sydow, J., Schreyog, G., & Koch, J. (2009). Organizational path dependence: Opening the black box. *The Academy of Management Review, 34*(4), 689–709.

Taylor, S., & Crocker, J. (1983). Schematic bases of social information processing. In E. Higgens, C. Herman, & J. Zauna (Eds.), *Social cognition: The Ontario symposium*. Hillsdale: Lawrence Erlbaum.

Teece, D., & Pisano, G. (1994). The dynamic capabilities of firms: An introduction. *Industrial and corporate change, 3*(3), 537–556.

Teece, D. J., Pisano, G., & Shuen, A. (1997). Dynamic capabilities and strategic management. *Strategic Management Journal, 18*(7), 509–533.

Tidd, J. (2001). Innovation management in context: Environment, organization and performance. *International Journal of Management Reviews, 3*(3), 169–183.

Tillquist, J., King, J. L., & Woo, C. (2002). A representational scheme for analyzing information technology and organizational dependency. *MIS Quarterly, 26*(2), 91–118.

Todd, P., & Benbasat, I. (1994). The influence of decision aids on choice strategies: An experimental analysis of the role of cognitive effort. *Organizational Behavior and Human Decision Processes, 60*(1), 36–74.

Tolman, E. (1948). Cognitive maps in rats and men. *Psychological Review, 1*(55), 189–208.

Turner, N., Swart, J., & Maylor, H. (2013). Mechanisms for managing ambidexterity: A review and research agenda. *International Journal of Management Reviews, 15*(3), 317–332.

Ulrich, D., & Barney, J. B. (1984). Perspectives in organizations: Resource dependence, efficiency, and population. *The Academy of Management Review, 9*(3), 471–481.

Vargo, S. L., & Lusch, R. F. (2004). Evolving to a new dominant logic for marketing. *Journal of marketing, 68*(1), 1–17.

Von Bertalanffy, L. (1972). The history and status of general systems theory. *Academy of Management Journal, 15*(4), 407–426.

Vroom, V. H., & Yetton, P. W. (1973). *Leadership and decision-making.* Pittsburgh: University of Pittsburgh Press.

Watts, D. J., & Strogatz, S. H. (1998). Collective dynamics of small-world networks. *Nature, 393*(6684), 440–442.

Weber, R. (1992). On the Gittins index for multiarmed bandits. *The Annals of Applied Probability, 2*(4), 1024–1033.

Weick, K. E. (1979). *The social psychology of organizing.* New York: McGraw-Hill.

Wernerfelt, B. (1984). A resource-based view of the firm. *Strategic Management Journal, 5*(2), 171–180.

Williamson, O. E. (1975). *Markets and hierarchies: Analysis and antitrust implications.* New York: Free Press.

Williamson, O. E. (1979). Transaction-cost economics: The governance of contractual relations. *The Journal of Law and Economics, 22*(2), 233–261.

Williamson, O. E. (1981). The economics of organization: The transaction cost approach. *American Journal of Sociology, 87*(3), 548–577.

Williamson, O. E. (1985). *The economic institutions of capitalism : Firms, markets, relational contracting.* New York: Free Press.

Winter, S. G. (2003). Understanding dynamic capabilities. *Strategic Management Journal, 24*(10), 991–995.

Winterhalter, S., Zeschky, M. B., & Gassmann, O. (2015). Managing dual business models in emerging markets: An ambidexterity perspective. *R&D Management, 4,* 464–479.

Zahra, S. A., & George, G. (2002). Absorptive capacity: A review, reconceptualization, and extension. *The Academy of Management Review, 27*(2), 185–203.

Zimmermann, A., Raisch, S., & Birkinshaw, J. (2015). How is ambidexterity initiated? The emergent charter definition process. *Organization Science, 26*(4), 1119–1139.

Zott, C., & Amit, R. (2007). Business model design and the performance of entrepreneurial firms. *Organization Science, 18*(2), 181–199.

Zott, C., & Amit, R. (2010). Business model design: An activity system perspective. *Long Range Planning, 43*(2–3), 216–226.

CHAPTER 4

Exploring Upcoming Theories for BMI Research: Enlightening the Dark Side of the Moon

Abstract Creativity in research occurs by looking at the same phenomenon through new eyes, that is, different perspectives can be uncovered through novel theoretical lenses. Thirty additional theories with potential for future research in exploring multiple aspects of business models are presented in this chapter. These theories, however, lead a niche existence in management science compared to the ones introduced in Chap. 3. The sections are structured similar to Chap. 3 by introducing each of the 30 theories separately and then highlighting avenues for future research. This approach contributes to business model research in exploring how scholars can profit by drawing on a broader array of theories. Analysing business models in management science seems like a paradigm shift in which new perspectives are needed to explore the phenomenon. This chapter provides a comprehensive foundation for this end.

Keywords Business models • Business model innovation • New theoretical views • Review of 30 niche theories in management science • Avenues for future research • Future research directions

4.1   Theory of Argumentation

The theory of argumentation is rooted in philosophical science and analyses the form and purpose of argumentation structures. The concept is linked to the key constructs of *logic* and builds on the reasoning of premises and conclusions. The theory is credited to Toulmin, who developed it for explaining everyday argumentations (Toulmin, 1958). The main components of Toulmin's model are the *data, warrant,* and *claim,* which together build an argumentation. In their description of an argument, Brockriede and Ehninger (1960) refer to Toulmin and describe an argument as 'movement from accepted data, through a warrant, to a claim' (p. 544). Toulmin's model of argumentation includes three additional parts: *backings,* which are the evidence or support of the warrants; *rebuttals,* which are the description of exceptions to the claim, and *qualifications,* which are limitations to the claim, warrant, and backing.

Consideration of this theory begs the question: why does an organization need a new business model? The most often cited arguments in favour of, and perhaps also against, BMIs, including the argumentation procedures to obtain the organization's whole commitment, need to be underlined using this theory. Future research may adapt the theory to analyse how successful lines of argumentation and reasoning should be designed, for instance, by exploring how senior management argumentation lines create a sense of urgency and legitimacy among middle management. Research in this field might also integrate a stakeholder management perspective, as can be seen in Sect. 3.19 later.[1]

4.2   Attention-Based View

In the spirit of Herbert Simon (1947) and the theory of administrative behaviour, theories gradually moved from rational choice approaches. Ocasio (1997), in attempting to explain organizations' decision-making processes, builds on the findings of human rationality. However, the *attention-based view* is also inspired by theories and empirical studies from the fields of social psychology, economics, and cognitive science. The attention-based view puts forward the idea of limited attentional capability of humans, which results from the bounded capacity of being rational (Ocasio, 1997). In Ocasio's eyes, attention is the scarcest of all resources. Thus, firm behaviour is explained by how organizations structure, distribute, and influence the attention of decision makers. Attention is directed to *issues* and *answers*, which may best be described by defining them as existing action alternatives or evidence on the environment.

The attention-based view cannot explain competitive advantages and does not replace previous theories, for example, the resource-based view (Ocasio, 1997). However, the theory is a strong tool to connect an organizational perspective with the individual level in firms. It can imply for business model research that, using the attention-based view, decision makers face the difficulty of *thinking outside the box* and innovating the business model not because of their lack of creativity or intellectual ability, but precisely due to the organizational structural distribution of their attention. For instance, Bock, Opsahl, George, and Gann (2012, p. 299) find that 'understanding how business model innovators achieve strategic flexibility requires a nuanced appreciation of the link between structural changes, managerial attention, and control.' In addition, research on business models may examine the conflict of long-term attention and therefore, more explorative business models, which is in contrast to the attention of middle management on short-term issues, such as exploitative initiatives. Ultimately, paying high attention to the external environment (e.g. venture and start-up activities), disruptive technological changes, or novel business model patterns are antecedents for business model innovation (BMI) and hence, may be topics for future study.

Micheli, Berchicci, Ocasio, and Jansen (2015) relate a 'managers' attention to their business models to the future implementation of BMI' (p. 8). In this way, a manager's individual attention may be seen as an antecedent of BMI as the manager's understanding of a business model relates to the ability to initiate BMI. Furthermore, BMI may only be successful if two facilitating factors are accomplished on an individual and organizational level: a multi-focal set plan and the creation of shared frames. Both lead to the attentional engagement to BMI (Micheli et al., 2015). Martins et al. (2015) come from a similar perspective and explore how firms may overcome inertia to innovate a business model in the absence of exogenous change (e.g. external technological change). In order to do so, the authors suggest that business models are a cognitive structure that organizes managerial understanding of internal and external interdependencies. In this vein, they argue that BMI takes place only through systematic cognitive processes and active attentional focus on new issues and answers. The authors propose that this attentional focus may be implemented by taking into account analogical reasoning and conceptual combination in a firm-level strategic process.[2]

4.3   Chaos Theory

Chaos theory describes the timely behaviour of systems with chaotic/deterministic dynamics. The theory builds on the fundamental finding that measurements are not perfectly precise. In particular, starting conditions cannot be specified with infinite accuracy and thus, unpredictable outcomes are the result. Building on this assumption, chaotic systems are afflicted with a high sensitivity to initial conditions. Initial inaccuracies or variations have a vast impact on the outcome, as imprecision propagates exponentially. A practical implication of chaos theory is that two nearly identical sets of initial conditions for the same system may result in significantly different outcomes, albeit within limits.

Adopting this theory to business model literature may be a difficult enterprise due to the complex task of taking measures in social sciences. However, basic assumptions and central ideas of the theory can inspire research topics. Companies in new markets often start with similar business models, yet these models differ slightly in a few important respects, and thus, have completely different starting conditions. By adopting chaos theory, a business will evolve completely differently. Research could enquire into which factors have the biggest impact by using longitudinal analysis or sensitivity analyses for BMI. Using longitudinal process analysis, research could evaluate the characteristics of BMI processes. This might become possible through the use of research designs developed by Van de Ven and Poole in Minnesota (Van de Ven & Poole, 1995).[3]

4.4   Competitive Imitation

The *theory of competitive imitation* explores a firm's behaviour, which mainly consists of copying attributes of other firms. Scholars in this field study the dynamics of imitation, attributes that are imitated, the efficacy of the search process, and the effects of imitation on firm and industry performance (Csaszar & Siggelkow, 2010; Ethiraj, Levinthal, & Roy, 2008; Ethiraj & Zhu, 2008; Posen et al., 2012; Rivkin, 2000). By imitating attributes of other firms, companies aim for a superior configuration of their extant status quo, sometimes even surpassing the industry leader. Subsequently, imitation may be defined as a search process by which a firm strives to copy attributes of a high-performing firm (Posen et al., 2012). By observing the effects of both strategic similarity and dissimilarity on firm performance, Deephouse (1999) develops a theory of *strategic balance*. According to his study, firms reduce competition through differentiation and enhance legitimacy through confirmation. Therefore, their goal is to strike a balance between being as dissimilar from competitors as possible while being capable of legitimizing their existence.

The business model may well be applied as a unit of analysis in imitation processes and thereby be regarded as means for innovation. Imitation has been found to be an important research stream in business model literature since BMI means—at least to a certain extent—differentiation from competitors. Teece (2010) argues that companies could adopt business models that have been spearheaded by a company in one industry and transfer it to another. Conceptually, this idea is in line with Baden-Fuller and Morgan (2010), who argue that business models may serve as recipes open to variation and innovation. Similarly, and by focusing on competitive imitation and business model imitation, Casadesus-Masanell and Zhu (2010, 2013) tackle this topic. In addition, Asapara, Hietanen, and Tikkanen (2009) study different outcomes of small and large firms. They find that firms put different emphasis on both BMI and replication. Ultimately, Enkel and Mezger (2013) link imitation to BMI activities and suggest a process of abstraction, analogy identification, and adaptation.[4]

4.5   Cognitive Dissonance Theory

Another theory based on cognitive psychology is *cognitive dissonance theory*, introduced by Leon Festinger in 1957. From a socio-psychological perspective, emotional states are perceived as unpleasant when the relationship between aspects of our cognition seem to be incompatible. For example, if a person's belief system or opinion significantly clashes with his decisions or actions, a dissonance and consequently, a stressful condition are aroused. The theory indicates the tendency of individuals to eliminate such inconsistencies; however, it is more likely that individuals change an attitude in order to accommodate the behaviour.

One may make use of cognitive dissonance theory in the field of business models to understand why it is so difficult for individuals to create and adapt cognitively dissonant, new ideas. What can be inferred from this theory is that people attempt to reduce dissonance by not accepting radically new business model ideas; that is, ideas which are not in line with the dominant logic of the industry and company. Analogously, cognitive dissonance theory might help to explain why entrepreneurs develop new business models or start their own businesses. In this regard, one could analyse their personal dissonance along with their motivation to start a new business.[5]

4.6   Social Cognitive Theory

Social cognitive theory is rooted in psychology research and at its core is a *learning theory.* A key statement of the theory is that people are products of their environment but also act as producers. In this sense, the theory investigates the extent to which individuals are influenced by others and their environment, and how they learn by observing the same. In contrast to classic approaches in psychology, focusing on unidirectional causation in which 'behaviour is depicted as being shaped and controlled either by environmental influences or by internal dispositions, social cognitive theory explains psychosocial functioning in terms of triadic reciprocal causation' (Wood & Bandura, 1989: p. 361). The three key constructs of *behaviour, cognitive/personal factors,* and *environmental events* now 'operate as interacting determinants that influence each other bi-directionally' (Wood & Bandura, 1989, p. 361).

Cognitive maps of managers can be influenced by patterns of business models in other industries. Social cognitive theory can explain how the cognitive maps and, consequently, the behaviour of managers and employees can be changed (for more details, see Baden-Fuller & Morgan, 2010). Tikkanen, Lamberg, Parvinen, and Kallunki's (2005) main finding is that a business model is essentially a cognitive phenomenon as well as built on the material aspects of a firm.[6]

4.7   Theory of Constraints

This theory is grounded in the proverb 'a chain is only as strong as its weakest link.' Corporate performance is not dictated by the highest performing person or part, but by constraints, which prevent the organization from achieving maximum performance and efficiency. The theory goes on to clarify the methodology of eliminating constraints, thereby using the following five steps: *identification, exploitation, subordination, elevation,* and *repetition* (Goldratt, 1990).

Habtay (2012) reasons that 'while the existing literature emphasizes financial valuation as a basis for drawing prospective investors and actors, (…) knowledge and social motives are equally important for drawing public actors in supporting a latent disruptive technology especially before its market unfolds' (p. 301). Thus, financial constraints must not necessarily impede BMI processes. The theory of constraints defines constraints not only as people but also as information, supplies, technology, equipment, and other organizational parts. Therefore, business model research could apply the same methodology to identify the weakest link of the business model and improve it in the same way managers would optimize their production teams. In particular, small and medium enterprises and start-ups with scarce resources could be analysed. How can resource-scarce companies configure new value networks? What are the most evident environmental constraints of the business model? Moreover, resource constraints could be analysed from a market perspective. How can business models be developed around frugal products for emerging markets? How can new business models for consumers at the bottom of the pyramid be addressed? (Winterhalter, Zeschky, & Gassmann, 2015).[7]

4.8   EFFECTUATION

Effectuation is the result of attempting scientific deconstruction of entrepreneurial behaviour and is the inverse of causation (Sarasvathy, 2008). Causation suggests that entrepreneurs adopt pre-existing goals which they strive to reach through means and ways they identify as necessary. By contrast, effectuation implies having pre-existing means, which entrepreneurs use to identify goals they can attain. In other words, entrepreneurs put emphasis on creating something new with pre-existing means, rather than achieving pre-existing goals through finding new means. The effectual model recognizes five principles (Sarasvathy, 2008): *patchwork quilt principle* (means-driven action), *affordable loss principle* (decision makers act according to what they can afford to lose, instead of what they expect to win), *bird-in-hand principle* (the principal negotiates and works with any stakeholder who shows commitment without thinking about opportunity costs or any other elaborate analysis), *lemonade principle* (the principal acknowledges surprises rather than avoids and overcomes them), and finally, *pilot-in-the-plane principle* (the principal focuses solely on what is controllable and doable, not on exogenous factors, such as socio-economic trends).

Chanal and Caron-Fasan's (2010) finding in their longitudinal study on open business models and crowdsourcing platforms shows that the business model is 'more of an ongoing learning process than a final result to be implemented through a business plan' (p. 337). This recalls the approach of effectuation to entrepreneurship, opposing *effectual reasoning* with *causal reasoning*. Furthermore, their study suggests *dynamic consistency*: in order to ensure the sustainability of a business model, the firm must have the capability to continuously change it. As Sarasvathy (2008) puts it, the effectual model changes the phrase 'to the extent we can predict the future, we can control it' into 'to the extent we can control the future, we do not need to predict it' (p. 17).

Effectuation is mainly rooted in entrepreneurship literature. For business model research, it could imply that innovation and change brought to the business model are not reactions to market changes and socio-economic megatrends but proactive measures by organizations putting emphasis on 'what can we do?' instead of 'what should we do?'[8]

4.9   EQUITY THEORY

Equity theory analyses how people strive for fairness within their interpersonal and social relationships. According to the theory, a person always compares their input (e.g. the contribution made by an employee for the organization) with the received output (e.g. the salary) to the input and output they observe for their peers. In the case of equilibrium, which means the employer feels equally treated compared to others, a person perceives fairness and is positively motivated. In the case of disequilibrium regarding the input–output ratio, which is less or greater than that of others, people become distressed and attempt to balance the situation through several different reactions.

The input required from employees during BMI implementation is very high. Equity theory may explain the incentive system behind BMI processes. Due to decisions and prospects that are perceived as unfair, change processes more often than not receive low support from individuals. The question that arises is whether sharing the potential profits of a BMI would motivate people to take a more active role in BMI within incumbents' firms. The theory might also be linked with the inducement–contribution model and the concept of organizational balance presented by March and Simon (1958). They state that for stakeholders to contribute to and participate in a company, they have to receive inducements (e.g. salary, interest rates, goods, and services). A business model should provide such a perceived balance of inducements and contributions in order to motivate stakeholders.[9]

4.10   EXPERIENTIAL LEARNING THEORY

Experiential Learning Theory emphasizes the central role that real-life experience plays in the learning process, differentiating itself from theories of cognitive and behavioural learning (Kolb, Boyatzis, & Mainemelis, 2001). Rather than replacing existing learning theories, experiential learning theory expands current approaches by simultaneously considering the entirety of perception, cognition, behaviour, and experience. By highlighting the central role of experience in the learning process, experiential learning theory gives a more holistic picture and integrative view.

Kolb et al. (2001) explain that learning requires opposite abilities, and that learners have to choose which set of learning abilities they will use in a learning situation (p. 228). Learners can absorb new information through experiencing the tangible and felt qualities of the surrounding environment, thereby relying only on their senses, whereas others can learn through symbolic representation and abstract conceptualization (reflection, analysis, and thought). Put differently, some prefer to carefully observe others who are involved in an experience, whereas others prefer jumping right into the experience and acting upon it (watchers vs. doers).

Khanagha, Volberda, and Oshri (2014) argue that strategy formation and business model configuration in a company need mutual experiential learning that revolves around different strategic intentions ranging from transformation of the business model to incremental improvements. Further significant potential for business model research can be pulled out of the theory by better understanding the *learning-by-doing* processes of change and project management. In this way, scholars may attempt to find a standardized framework or model of easing improvisation activities during the implementation phase of BMI. Moreover, the importance of experimenting with *minimal viable products* and *rapid prototyping* is gradually gaining more attention in business, particularly among practitioners and scholars of entrepreneurship (Thomke & Manzi, 2014).[10]

4.11   FLOW THEORY

Flow theory is a concept developed by Csikszentmihalyi (1975). It is strongly interwoven with the concept of intrinsic motivation. It describes a mental state of focused attention and total engagement. Although a flow is conceptually defined as 'the holistic experience that people feel when they act with total involvement' (Csikszentmihalyi, p. 36), flow access and flow experience are very specific to each person. To enable a flow experience, three key premises must be met: an activity has a clear objective, a high concentration on the action is aroused, and a task and skills demanded are in accordance, in order to avoid both boredom and overload.

Creating and maintaining work and information flow within a team in the business model design and ideation phase are vital subjects of research. Using flow theory, the conditions and antecedents of flows within BMI teams may be identified for further improvement.[11]

4.12   GAME THEORY

Game Theory is an area of applied mathematics used by various disciplines (e.g. economics, military, evolutionary biology, and political science). In short, the theory deals with the modelling of decision-making situations within formalized incentive structures (games). The key criterion for delimiting game theory from decision theory is that decisions are made in an environment in which various actors act strategically. Hence, costs and benefits of a decision strongly depend upon the behaviour of other parties. In order to find an optimal strategy, game theory studies the predicted and actual behaviour of other parties in a game.

Casadesus-Masanell and Zhu (2010) conduct a game-theoretical experiment in order to determine how competitive actions through BMI affect the business models of competitors. Their study focuses on four generic business model patterns: *subscription-based, ad-sponsored, mixed,* and *dual models.* Game theory can be very helpful to analyse potential interactions and strategic moves of the relevant actors within an ecosystem. Innovations brought to business models are certainly the results of careful strategic analysis of the business environment, and the extrapolation of potential responses and moves made by competitors and customers.[12]

4.13   GARBAGE CAN THEORY

As a counter-movement to approaches that build on structured patterns to explain decision-making in organizations, this theory broaches the issue of the highly ambivalent and complex traits of reality. The term *organized anarchies* is introduced as the *garbage can theory* and attempts to describe non-rational decision-making processes. Three main properties that often have been empirically identified in organizational studies characterize an organized anarchy. The first is *problematic preferences* (e.g. problems and goals are not clearly defined), the second raises the role of *unclear technologies* (e.g. organizational parameters and structures are not communicated, and means–end relationships remain unclear), and the third is the issue of *fluid participation* (e.g. participants of the decision-making process change regularly, and the engagement of people is highly dependent on their individual motivation and commitment). Organized anarchies trigger situations in which problems are uncoupled from choices and a project or team seems to be *rummaging around* inside a garbage can.

The garbage-can decision setting can be used to describe and analyse collective decision-making processes in BMIs. Such a decision can be of an intra-organizational or an inter-organizational nature. The latter especially has not been investigated yet.[13]

4.14   THEORY OF ILLUSION OF CONTROL

The *theory of illusion of control* is proposed by Langer and Roth (1975). A central insight is that humans tend to perceive situations as controllable although an individual is not in a position to manipulate the specific situation. A prominent example is the case of people estimating their winning chances in a lottery as being higher when picking the numbers personally rather than using a random generator. Although the illusion of control was first studied given situations partially determined by chance, it could be even better applied to situations of both chance and skill-driven activities. This is because individuals are prone to overconfidence in collaborative situations.

Even though it is not possible to control all external influencing factors of a firm, BMI processes still provide managers with a certain illusion of control, as the business model design process shapes the company in accordance with new trends and competitive requirements. An interesting pathway for research is to identify which business models of companies use personal behaviour marked by the illusion of customers and how they do so.[14]

4.15   INFORMATION-PROCESSING THEORY

Information-processing theory forms part of cognitive psychology. It involves analysis of human memory and as such, the storage of information and retrieval of knowledge. Human cognitive mechanisms are considered information-processing actions that centre on recording, retaining, and operating knowledge. A key contribution and widely accepted framework is proposed by Atkinson and Shiffrin (1968) as *stage theory*. According to the model, information is processed and stored in three stages—the sensory memory, the short-term memory, and the long-term memory. Several other theories support information-processing theory and the Atkinson and Shiffrin model. For instance, George A. Miller (1956) provides the theoretical finding of *chunking*, which claims that the capacity of the short-term memory is reduced to hold seven (+/– two) chunks of information (a chunk is any meaningful unit: a word, a person's face, a name, or a number).

Information-processing theory is helpful for analysing business models in the context of individual and organizational capabilities of processing required information on the business model ecosystem. Special emphasis of future research could be placed on the relationship of central/corporate units towards decentralized business units in the development and processing of business model information.[15]

4.16   Language Action Perspective

Conventional theories are based on the assumption that communication is a way of exchanging information. The language action perspective (LAP) goes further to state that language is used to initiate and perform actions (e.g. Flores & Ludlow, 1980). Putting *language* in this light, communication must be given significant importance in an organizational context to understand how people and divisions communicate with each other in order to coordinate activities. LAP scholars point out that effective information technology systems have to be adjusted according to an LAP, as the purpose of IT is to support an organization's communication system. It becomes indispensable to consider a linguistic perspective as proposed by Winograd (2006) and Schoop (2001).

Every industry is characterized by jargon, which creates the context of its actors. Changing business models require challenging existing languages and creating new languages. This is especially relevant when business model practices are transferred from one industry to another or when industries converge. Another aspect addresses the role of languages in realizing change for BMI implementation in the organization.[16]

4.17   MANAGEMENT FASHION THEORY

Management fashion theory analyses how companies focus on and apply management innovation models from *fashion setting organizations* (e.g. consulting firms and business schools). Fashions are considered managerial techniques, such as the *management by objectives* or *total quality management* methods. Management fashion theory implies that fashions become institutionalized because of socio-psychological factors rather than by rationally or technically reasoned decisions. It examines the process of emergence and decline of fashions in an uncertain environment. One crucial focus of investigation is why a small minority of concepts find wide acceptance over a longer time of period, whereas a great majority emerges and declines quickly; according to Abrahamson (1991), these fashions are called *fads*.

Some business models, which are used by fashion-setting organizations, for example, Google, are imitated more often than others, and therefore, spread more quickly across different industries. Business model researchers can use this theory to explain the drivers of business model diffusion and recommend which business model patterns are more likely to be used or underused for this reason. In fact, some critics might consider the term 'business model' or 'BMI' itself to be a fashion in management research and practice.[17]

4.18   NEW INSTITUTIONALISM

While *old institutionalism* is concerned with the study of how institutions emerge and function, *new institutionalism*, introduced by Meyer and Rowan (1977), explains that institutions should not only justify their existence economically but also justify their legitimacy within the institutional environment in order to continue to exist (institutional peer pressure). From this point of view, an institution's main goal is to survive. Institutions make decisions on the basis of how they can maximize benefits (regulative institutionalism), of what they are supposed to do (normative institutionalism), and of the founding reason that they have no other choices they can conceive of (cognitive institutionalism). The BMI's goal is for managers to force break-up through the observation of cognitive institutionalism (institutions act and decide because they cannot think of any other alternatives).[18]

4.19   ORGANIZATIONAL CULTURE THEORY

Organizational culture theory has many facets as several powerful theoretical frameworks in academic literature exist. In short, *culture* always manifests itself in values, norms, or beliefs. Common to all approaches is the analysis of how culture influences institutional performance and organizational goals. Either culture may be considered as something that an organization possesses (functionalist view) or the organization itself may be considered a culture (interpretivist view). The widest accepted framework is established by Schein (1990) (functionalist view), who defines culture as an organizing framework. In that way, culture is a 'pattern of basic assumptions – invented, discovered, or developed by a given group (…) that has worked well enough to be considered valid and, therefore, to be taught to new members as the correct way to perceive, think, and feel in relation to (…) problems' (p. 111).

Organizational culture theory can explain which organizations are more likely to innovate their business model and which are stuck in a pattern of basic assumptions. Managers have to change structures to initiate innovation (Hall & Saias, 1980). For instance, Bock et al. (2012) explain in a quantitative study that a creative culture enables the strategic flexibility when firms start BMI.[19]

4.20   ORGANIZATIONAL INFORMATION-PROCESSING THEORY

Organizational information processing theory (OIPT) relates to the question of how to structure firms for effective and efficient performance. According to OIPT, the most significant determinant in structuring a company is uncertainty, both task and environmental uncertainty. For instance, a high degree of uncertainty requires a greater amount of information processing. Basically, there are two concepts to cope with uncertainty—the first is to reduce the need for information processing (e.g. creation of buffers and self-contained tasks). The second is to increase the capability of information processing (e.g. establishment of structural mechanisms to reduce uncertainty as investment in information systems or creation of lateral relations as improvement of information flow).

Business model research can use this theory to investigate the required capabilities of an organization to innovate its business model. The cognitive distance of the old and new business models has to fit the organizational information-processing capabilities of an organization.[20]

4.21 PORTFOLIO THEORY

The chief objective of *portfolio theory* is to explore the right allocation of assets. In order to achieve an optimal portfolio, investors have to find a balance between the minimization of risk and maximization of returns. Almost every portfolio selection strategy builds on the work of Markowitz (1952), who won the Nobel Prize for his concept in 1990. He structures a portfolio in strategic/passive asset allocation and tactical/active asset allocation. Although the concepts of portfolio theory have been widely accepted in theory and practice, recent developments, such as the financial crisis or advancements in behavioural economics, have revealed limitations.

Research could address the valuation issues of business models. For example, are firms that develop and manage various and distinct BMI initiatives more successful than focused firms? In addition, it should be noted that companies apply different business models at different levels (hierarchical levels, project-based levels, etc.) and in several different divisions. These different BMI processes may be considered as a portfolio of projects that could be handled by the financial portfolio theory.[21]

4.22 PRODUCT LIFECYCLE MODEL

The *product lifecycle model* describes the process of managing the entire lifecycle of a product, typically recognized as the following five phases (Stark, 2011): *ideation, definition, realization, usage*, and *disposal*. The lifecycle phases can be categorized into three groups: *beginning of life*, (ideation, definition, and realization), *middle of life* (support, maintenance, usage, and servicing), and *end of life* (retirement and disposal). The goal is to maximize the product revenue and product portfolio value and to minimize product-related costs.

If business models were to be considered as a *product*, then it implies that business models have a lifecycle. Just like an automaker would constantly release face-lifted versions or fully new models of its line-up, it should be then considered that managers should perpetually replace business models with new or updated ones, each with its own *date of expiration*. Analogously, it would be highly interesting to research the timing of BMI processes during the product lifecycle model (Zollenkop, 2008). Furthermore, it would be highly interesting to study how different business model patterns are applied along a product's lifecycle or even along the industry lifecycle. Commoditized products require patterns such as solution bundles or pay-per-unit models with a high servitization rather than one time payments (Cusumano, Kahl, & Suarez, 2015).[22]

4.23   Prospect Theory

Prospect theory forms part of behavioural economics and replaces the assumption of the completely rational individual (homo economicus) with a model that takes pervasive effects and human bias into consideration. Kahneman and Tversky (1979) identify several aspects of cognitive bias that invalidate the *expected utility theory*. For instance, humans are motivated more strongly by losses than gains as they put more energy in the avoidance of losses. Furthermore, empirical findings have discovered the certainty, reflection, and isolation effects. In accordance with the certainty effect, Kahneman and Tversky argue that people focus more on outcomes obtained with certainty than on merely probable outcomes. This leads individuals to be more risk averse in secure choices and more risk seeking in choices involving losses (Kahneman & Tversky, 1979). Prospect theory emerged as a critique of expected utility theory and is considered a *psychologically more realistic* concept.

Prospect theory is relevant for researching the behavioural elements of stopping a BMI initiative. Issues like sunk costs, including investments, within organizational theory can be examined from a perspective of pathological individual decision. Dewald and Bowen (2010) present a cognitive perspective on how managers react to disruptive BMI opportunities. The answer could be inaction, resilience, adoption, or proactive resistance. Their study uses cognitive framing 'to predict when small incumbents would exhibit each of the four responses to disruptive innovation' (Dewald & Bowen, 2010, p. 213).[23]

4.24   Punctuated Equilibrium Theory

The *theory of punctuated equilibrium* stems from the research of Eldredge and Gould (1972) in the field of palaeontology. The theory provides an explanation for discontinuities in the evolution of species. The term *stasis* has been introduced to describe a period of stagnancy regarding evolutionary changes. Punctuation refers to the initiation of a short period of radical changes. In this spirit, the theory provides an antagonistic view to phyletic gradualism, which proposes a continuous process of changes. Gersick (1991) translates the theory into general management and claims that organizational structures remain unchanged during stasis but are deeply affected at punctuation due to fundamental environmental changes. The example of technological discontinuities serves as an analogy for revolutionary periods triggered by disruptive innovations and a new dominant logic (Anderson & Tushman, 1990; Romanelli & Tushman, 1994).

The punctuated equilibrium theory can help to understand when and how to overcome a business paradigm or dominant industry logic in the context of organizational behaviour. Environmental changes and technological discontinuities are key triggers for destroying the current equilibrium and thereby current business models. Habtay's (2012) study compares market-driven and technology-driven business models and finds that technology-induced business models follow forecasts of disruptive innovation theory and strategy. The findings show that in the short term, potential for technology-driven innovation is constrained by technological and market uncertainties, inferior value propositions, low-end niche markets, economic infeasibility, and resource scarcity. By contrast, 'market-driven innovations grow quickly and disrupt a significant part of the established mainstream market' (p. 299). In the long term, however, technology-driven innovations trump market-driven ones. Sabatier et al. (2012) characterize the term 'dominant industry logic' as follows. Even if technological breakthroughs are introduced, the dominant industry logic remains. A new industry logic develops slowly only after some time.[24]

4.25   REAL OPTIONS THEORY

Real options theory is a concept that extends corporate financial theory to real non-financial assets. According to Amram and Kulatilaka (1998), an option is the right, but not the obligation, to take an action in the future (commonly a strategic decision). The approach is highly valuable under uncertain conditions as it considers the aspects of rapid change and risk assessment. By applying financial methods to *real options*, strategic values for decisions are quantified. In a project setting, several options, such as redeploying, modifying, delaying, or even abandoning the project, are quantified as environmental and internal changes occur.

The real options approach is helpful to evaluate business models in which traditional financial approaches fail due to uncertainty. Future research could further formalize existing methods and practices of real options thinking in the business model field.[25]

4.26   SELF-EFFICACY THEORY

The *theory of self-efficacy* states that psychological procedures of any form strengthen and improve self-efficacy (Bandura, 1977). It distinguishes between outcome expectancy (a person's estimate that a given behaviour will lead to certain outcomes') and the more important efficacy expectancy (what the individual perceives to be his ability to execute the behaviour required for the outcome). The perceived self-efficacy influences an individual's behaviour; people behave more assuredly when believing they are capable of handling a situation and generally avoid circumstances which seem to exceed their coping skills (Bandura, 1982).

The effect of self-efficacy in BMI teams on the performance of BMI has not been examined sufficiently. Moreover, it would be interesting to examine the impact of leadership styles in BMI initiatives on self-efficacy and performance indicators.[26]

4.27   SLACK THEORY

In the field of organizational theory, *slack theory* explains the 'cushion of actual or potential resource which allows an organization to adapt successfully to internal pressures (…) to external pressures (…) as well as to initiate changes in strategy' (Bourgeois, 1981, p. 30). Slack is observed to be an intentional investment for long-term survival. However, it is criticized for being a source of organizational inefficiency.

Since slack forms the cushion that is necessary for organizations to safely navigate through times of pressure, slack theory may complement business model research by defining the amount of cost to be expected and planned for in BMI implementation.[27]

4.28   SOCIAL EXCHANGE THEORY

A key motivation for Homans (1958), the forefather of *social exchange theory*, to develop this new concept was to bring sociology closer to economics. In this spirit, the theory is set at the particular intersection of these fields, and is also influenced by psychology. In line with Blau's (1955) early work, the theory builds on the analogy that social behaviour is always an 'exchange of goods, material goods, but also non-material goods, such as symbols of approval or prestige' (Homans, 1958, p. 606). An exchange is based on the act of giving and taking, or in terms of social exchange theory, is defined by costs but rewarding of the reactions of the counterpart. According to Homans (1958), an individual seeks maximum profit in such exchanges, 'but he tries to see to it that no one in his group makes more profit than he does' (p. 606). Consequently, an individual's behaviour will not change if the profit of the social exchange tends to a maximum. Homans (1958) further implies that depending on the quantity of what an individual gives or receives, the cost and value of what he gives or receives will vary.

All business model concepts with markets as the central construct can be analysed and further developed by social exchange theory. In the ideation phase of business model development, social exchange theory might help to understand and lower the barriers that prevent people in a brainstorming process from contributing and sharing all their knowledge and ideas. Such a process might thereby be impeded if a participant feels he has drawn maximum profit out of a solution or attempts to hinder others from gaining more personal profit.[28]

4.29 STRUCTURATION THEORY

Structuration theory originates from the group of social theories. Whereas the similar term *structuralism* emphasizes the pre-eminence of the social entirety over its components, structuration theory in contrast relates to the interplay and relation of the individual (actor) and society (structure). According to Giddens (1979, p. 84), social structures are created, reproduced and therefore constituted by human behaviour (actors). Moreover, actions of the individual are not constrained by the structure but enabled by the latter (duality of structure). Put differently, 'social phenomena are not the product of either structure or agency, but of both (...) human agents draw on social structures in their actions, and at the same time these actions serve to produce and reproduce social structure' (Jones & Karsten, 2008, p. 129).

Adopting the theory on management and information systems science, DeSanctis and Poole (1994) used Giddens' theory to study the influence that advanced information systems have on the social organization of a firm and suggest the *Adaptive structuration theory* (AST). There is an interplay of the technology's structure and the emergent structure of the organization as well as social action: In a nutshell 'AST argues that advanced information technologies trigger adaptive structurational processes which, over time, can lead to changes in the rules and resources that organizations use in social interaction' (DeSanctis & Poole, 1994, pp. 142–143). For example, perceptions on the role and utility of information technology vary strongly across groups in organizations. In consequence, technology is used differently and thereby mediates the impact on group outcomes.

In business model research, structuration theory may help to overcome orthodoxies in an organization. Orthodoxies as common values and beliefs are barriers for an organization which intends to break the dominant logic of an industry. With the extension of DeSanctis and Poole (1994) on the use of modern information technology, business model research could use the theory to explain the role of virtual, IT-enabled teams in BMI of multinational companies.[29]

4.30   Transactive Memory Theory

Transactive memory theory sheds the light on other individuals serving as external memory in addition to our individual memory. Put differently, other individuals act as a location of external storage. According to Wegner (1986), a transactive memory system 'is a set of individual memory systems in combination with the communication that takes place between individuals' (p. 186). In this sense, transactive memories are properties of a group and by analysing and understanding how groups store and retrieve information, the behaviour of groups (or even group members) may be predicted. Groups tend to develop a working transactive memory where knowledge is encoded, stored, and retrieved by the collectivity and 'when the group is called upon to remember something, information is channelled to the known experts' (Wegner, p. 89). Empirical findings have shown that transactive memories are facilitators for group performance.

In entrepreneurial settings, founders or new venture teams can benefit from the encoded knowledge—*who knows what*—on their existing partner network. In the new light of effectuation, these assets can be used to close business model relevant knowledge gaps. In sum and by extending the concept of transactive memory theory, the acquisition of external knowledge for business models may be brought up. Often, there is a complementary interplay between internal and external knowledge for value creation as is outlined by Denicolai, Ramirez, and Tidd (2014).[30]

Notes

1. Main Literature: (Toulmin, 1958), (Brockriede & Ehninger, 1960).
2. Main Literature: (Simon, 1947), (Ocasio, 1997), (Cho & Hambrick, 2006), (Ocasio, 2011).
3. Main Literature: (Mandelbrot, 1983), (Gleich, 1987), (Cambel, 1993), (Robertson & Combs, 1995), (Van de Ven & Poole, 1995), (Thompson & Stewart, 2002).

4. Main Literature: (Deephouse, 1999), (Rivkin, 2000), (Ethiraj & Zhu, 2008), (Ethiraj, Levinthal & Roy, 2008), (Csaszar & Siggelkow, 2010), (Posen, Lee & Yi, 2012).
5. Main Literature: (Festinger, 1957), (Festinger & Carlsmith, 1959), (Brehm & Cohen, 1962), (Wicklund & Brehm, 1976).
6. Main Literature: (Bandura, 1977), (Bandura, 1986), (Bandura, 1989), (Jones, 1989), (Wood & Bandura, 1989), (Bandura, 2001).
7. Main Literature: (Goldratt, 1990), (Dettmer, 1997), (Rahman, 1998).
8. Main Literature: (Sarasvathy, 2001), (Sarasvathy, 2008).
9. Main Literature: (Homans, 1961), (Adams, 1963), (Adams, 1965), (Walster, Berscheid, & Walster, 1973), (Huseman, Hatfield, & Miles, 1987).
10. Main literature: (Kolb, 1984), (Kolb, Boyatzis & Mainemelis, 2001).
11. Main Literature: (Csikszentmihalyi, 1975), (Montgomery, Sharafi, & Hedman, 2004), (Qiu & Benbasat, 2005), (Hoffman & Novak, 2009).
12. Main Literature: (Morgenstern & Von Neumann, 1944), (Aumann & Schelling, 2005).
13. Main Literature: (Cohen, March, & Olsen, 1972).
14. Main Literature: (Langer, 1975), (Langer & Roth, 1975), (Presson & Benassi, 1996).
15. Main Literature: (Miller, 1956), (Miller, Galanter, & Pribram, 1960), (Atkinson & Shiffrin, 1968), (Zellner, 1988).
16. Main Literature: (Flores & Ludlow, 1980), (Goldkuhl & Lyytinen, 1982), (Lyytinen, 1985), (Winograd & Flores, 1986), (Schoop, 2001), (Winograd, 2006).
17. Main Literature: (Abrahamson, 1991), (Abrahamson, 1996), (Carson et al., 1999).
18. Main Literature: (Meyer & Rowan, 1977).
19. Main Literature: (Pettigrew, 1979), (Smircich, 1983), (Schein, 1985), (Schein, 2010).
20. Main Literature: (Galbraith, 1973), (Galbraith, 1974), (Premkumar, Ramamurthy, & Saunders, 2005).
21. Main Literature: (Markowitz, 1952), (McFarlan, 1981), (Karababas & Cather, 1994).
22. Main Literature: (Stark, 2011), (Cusumano, Kahl & Suarez, 2015).
23. Main Literature: (Kahneman & Tversky, 1979), (Tversky & Kahneman, 1981), (Kahneman & Tversky, 1984), (Bazerman, 1984), (Whyte, 1986), (Dewald & Bowen, 2010).
24. Main Literature: (Eldredge & Gould, 1972), (Hannan & Freeman, 1977), (Tushman & Romanelli, 1985), (Tushman & Anderson, 1986), (Gersick, 1991), (Romanelli & Tushman, 1994), (Lichtenstein, 1995), (Christensen, 2006).

25. Main Literature: (Myers, 1977), (Bookstaber, 1981), (Luehrman, 1998), (Amram & Kulatilaka, 1998).
26. Main Literature: (Bandura, 1977), (Bandura, 1978), (Bandura, 1982), (Compeau & Higgins, 1995a), (Compeau & Higgins, 1995b), (Bandura, 1997).
27. Main Literature: (Bourgeois, 1981), (Daniel et al., 2004)
28. Main Literature: (Blau, 1955), (Homans, 1958), (Levine & White, 1961), (Emerson, 1962), (Blau, 1964), (Cook, 1977).
29. Main Literature: (Giddens, 1979), (1984), (1991), (DeSanctis & Poole, 1994), (Jones & Karsten, 2008).
30. Main Literature: (Wegner, 1986), (Peltokorpi, 2008), (Lewis & Herndon, 2011), (Ren & Argote, 2011).

BIBLIOGRAPHY

Abrahamson, E. (1991). Managerial fads and fashions: The diffusion and refection of innovations. *Academy of Management Review, 16*(3), 586–612.

Abrahamson, E. (1996). Management fashion. *Academy of Management Review, 21*(1), 254–285.

Abrahamson, E., & Fairchild, G. (1999). Management fashion: Lifecycles, triggers, and collective learning processes. *Academy of Management Best Papers Proceedings, 44*(4), 708–740.

Adams, J. S. (1963). Towards an understanding of inequity. *Journal of Abnormal and Normal Social Psychology, 67*(5), 422–436.

Adams, J. S. (1965). Inequity in social exchange. *Advances in Experimental Social Psychology, 2*(4), 267–299.

Amram, M., & Kulatilaka, N. (1998). *Real options: Managing strategic investment in an uncertain world, OUP catalogue.* Oxford: Oxford University Press.

Anderson, P., & Tushman, M. L. (1990). Technological discontinuities and dominant designs : A cyclical model of technological change. *Administrative Science Quarterly, 35*(4), 604–633.

Aspara, J., Hietanen, J., & Tikkanen, H. (2009). Business model innovation vs. replication: Financial performance implications of strategic emphases. *Journal of Strategic Marketing, 18*(1), 39–56.

Atkinson, R. C., & Shiffrin, R. M. (1968). Human memory: A proposed system and its control processes. In K. Spence & J. Spence (Eds.), *Psychology of learning and motivation* (Vol. 2, pp. 89–195). New York: Academic.

Aumann, R.J., Schelling, T.C., Schelling, Thomas C. Nobelprize (2005). *Robert Aumann's and Thomas Schelling's Contributions to Game Theory: Analyses of Conflict and Cooperation.* Press release on scientific background, retrieved from: http://www.nobelprize.org/nobel_prizes/economic-sciences/laureates/2005/advanced-economicsciences2005.pdf

Baden-Fuller, C., & Morgan, M. S. (2010). Business models as models. *Long Range Planning, 43*(2–3), 156–171.

Bandura, A. (1977). Self-efficacy: Toward a unifying theory of behavioral change. *Psychological Review, 84*(2), 191–215.

Bandura, A. (1978). Reflections on self-efficacy. *Advances in Behaviour Research and Therapy, 1*(4), 237–269.

Bandura, A. (1982). Self-efficacy mechanism in human agency. *American Psychologist, 37*(2), 122–147.

Bandura, A. (1986). *Social foundations of thought and action: A social cognitive theory*. Englewood Cliffs: Prentice Hall.

Bandura, A. (1989). Human agency in social cognitive theory. *The American Psychologist, 44*(9), 1175–1184.

Bandura, A. (1997). *Self-efficacy: The exercise of control*. New York: W.H. Freeman and Co..

Bandura, A. (2001). Social cognitive theory: An agentic perspective. *Annual Review of Psychology, 52*(1), 1–26.

Bazerman, M. H. (1984). The relevance of Khaneman and Tversky's concept of framing to organization behavior. *Journal of Management, 10*(3), 333–343.

Blau, P. M. (1955). *The dynamics of bureaucracy*. Chicago: University of Chicago Press.

Blau, P. M. (1964). *Exchange and power in social life*. New York: Wiley.

Bock, A. J., Opsahl, T., George, G., & Gann, D. M. (2012). The effects of culture and structure on strategic flexibility during business model innovation. *Journal of Management Studies, 49*(2), 279–305.

Bookstaber, R. M. (1981). *Option pricing and strategies in investing*. Boston: Addison-Wesley.

Bourgeois, L. J. (1981). On the measurement of organizational slack. *The Academy of Management Review, 6*(1), 29–39.

Brehm, J. W., & Cohen, A. R. (1962). *Explorations in cognitive dissonance*. New York: Wiley.

Brockriede, W., & Ehninger, D. (1960). Toulmin on argument: An interpretation and application. *Quarterly Journal of Speech, 46*(1), 44–53.

Cambel, A. B. (1993). *Applied chaos theory-A paradigm for complexity*. Boston: Academic.

Carson, P. P., Lanier, P. A., Carson, K. D., & Birkenmeier, B. J. (1999). A historical perspective on fad adoption and abandonment. *Journal of Management History, 5*(6), 320–333.

Casadesus-Masanell, R., & Zhu, F. (2013). Business model innovation and competitive imitation: The case of sponsor-based business models. *Strategic Management Journal, 34*(4), 464–482.

Chanal, V., & Caron-Fasan, M.-L. (2010). The difficulties involved in developing business models open to innovation communities: The case of a crowdsourcing platform. *M@n@gement, 13*(4), 318–341.

Cho, T. S., & Hambrick, D. C. (2006). Attention as the mediator between top management team characteristics and strategic change: The case of airline deregulation. *Organization Science, 17*(4), 453–469.

Christensen, C. M. (2006). The ongoing process of building a theory of disruption. *Journal of Product Innovation Management, 23*(1), 39–55.

Cohen, M. D., March, J. G., & Olsen, J. P. (1972). A garbage can model of organizational choice. *Administrative Science Quarterly, 17*(1), 1–25.

Compeau, D. R., & Higgins, C. A. (1995a). Application of social cognitive theory to training for computer skills. *Information Systems Research, 6*(2), 118–143.

Compeau, D. R., & Higgins, C. A. (1995b). Computer self-efficacy: Development of a measure and initial test. *MIS Quarterly, 19*(2), 189–211.

Cook, K. S. (1977). Exchange and power in networks of interoganizational relations. *The Sociological Quarterly, 18*(1), 62–82.

Csaszar, F. A., & Siggelkow, N. (2010). How much to copy? Determinants of effective imitation breadth. *Organization Science, 21*(3), 661–676.

Csikszentmihalyi, M. (1975). Play and intrinsic rewards. *Journal of Humanistic Psychology, 15*(3), 41–63.

Cusumano, M. A., Kahl, S. J., & Suarez, F. F. (2015). Services, industry evolution, and the competitive strategies of product firms. *Strategic Management Journal, 36*(4), 559–575.

Daniel, F., Lohrke, F. T., Fornaciari, C. J., & Turner, R. A. (2004). Slack resources and firm performance: A meta-analysis. *Journal of Business Research., 57*(6), 565–574.

Deephouse, D. L. (1999). To be different, or to be the same? It's a question (and theory) of strategic balance. *Strategic Management Journal, 20*(2), 147–166 http://doi.org/10.2307/3094023.

Denicolai, S., Ramirez, M., & Tidd, J. (2014). Creating and capturing value from external knowledge: The moderating role of knowledge intensity. *R&D Management, 44*(3), 248–264.

DeSanctis, G., & Poole, M. (1994). Capturing the complexity in advanced technology use: Adaptive structuration theory. *Organization Science, 5*(2), 121–147.

Dettmer, H. W. (1997). *Goldratt's theory of constraints: A systems approach to continuous improvement.* Milwaukee: ASQ Quality Press.

Dewald, J., & Bowen, F. (2010). Storm clouds and silver linings: Responding to disruptive innovations through cognitive resilience. *Entrepreneurship Theory and Practice, 34*(1), 197–218.

Eldredge, N., & Gould, S. (1972). Punctuated equilibria: An alternative to phyletic gradualism. In T. J. Schopf (Ed.), *Models in paleobiology* (pp. 82–115). San Francisco: Freeman, Cooper & Co..

Emerson, R. M. (1962). Power-dependence relations. *American Sociological Review, 27*(1), 31–41.

Enkel, E., & Mezger, F. (2013). Imitation processes and their application for business model innovation: An explorative study. *International Journal of Innovation Management*, *17*(01) , 5–39.

Ethiraj, S. K., & Zhu, D. H. (2008). Performance effects of imitative entry. *Strategic Management Journal*, *29*(8), 797–817.

Ethiraj, S. K., Levinthal, D., & Roy, R. R. (2008). The dual role of modularity: Innovation and imitation. *Management Science*, *54*(5), 939–955.

Festinger, L. (1957). *A theory of cognitive dissonance*. Stanford: Stanford University Press.

Festinger, L., & Carlsmith, J. M. (1959). Cognitive consequences of forced compliance. *The Journal of Abnormal and Social Psychology*, *58*(2), 203–210.

Flores, F., & Ludlow, J. (1980). Doing and speaking in the office. In G. Fick & R. H. Sprague (Eds.), *Decision support systems: Issues and challenges* (pp. 95–118). New York: Pergamon Press.

Galbraith, J. R. (1973). *Designing complex organizations*. Boston: Addison-Wesley.

Galbraith, J. R. (1974). Organization design: An information processing view. *Interfaces*, *4*(3), 28–36.

Gersick, C. (1991). Revolutionary change theories: A multilevel exploration of the punctuated equilibrium paradigm. *The Academy of Management Review*, *16*(1), 10–36.

Giddens, A. (1979). *Central problems in social theory: Action, structure, and contradiction in social analysis*. Berkeley: University of California Press.

Giddens, A. (1984). *The constitution of society: Outline of the theory of structuration*. Berkeley: University of California Press.

Giddens, A. (1991). Structuration theory: Past, present and future. In C. G. A. Bryant & D. Jary (Eds.), *Giddens' theory of structuration. A critical appreciation* (pp. 201–221). London: Routledge.

Gleich, J. (1987). *Chaos: Making a new science*. New York: Viking.

Goldkuhl, G., & Lyytinen, K. (1982). A language action view of information systems. In: *International conference on information systems*.

Goldratt, E. M. (1990). *Theory of constraints*. Croton-on-Hudson: North River.

Habtay, S. R. (2012). A firm-level analysis on the relative difference between technology-driven and market-driven disruptive business model innovations. *Creativity and Innovation Management*, *21*(3), 290–303.

Hall, D., & Saias, M. (1980). Strategy follows structure! *Strategic Management Journal*, *1*(2), 149–163.

Hannan, M. T., & Freeman, J. (1977). The population ecology of organizations. *American Journal of Sociology*, *82*(5), 929–964.

Hoffman, D. L., & Novak, T. P. (2009). Flow online: Lessons learned and future prospects. *Journal of Interactive Marketing*, *23*(1), 23–34.

Homans, G. C. (1958). Social behavior as exchange. *American Journal of Sociology,* *63*(6), 597–606.

Homans, G. C. (1961). *Social behavior: Its elementary forms.* New York: Harcourt.

Huseman, R. C., Hatfield, J. D., & Miles, E. W. (1987). A new perspective on equity theory: The equity sensitivity construct. *Academy of Management Review, 12*(2), 222–234.

Jones, J. W. (1989). Personality and epistemology: Cognitive social learning theory as a philosophy of science. *Zygon, 24*(1), 23–38.

Jones, M. R., & Karsten, H. (2008). Giddens's structuration theory and information systems research. *MIS Quarterly, 32*(1), 127–157.

Kahneman, D., & Tversky, A. (1979). Prospect theory: An analysis of decision under risk. *Econometrica, 47*(2), 263–291.

Kahneman, D., & Tversky, A. (1984). Choices, values, and frames. *American Psychologist, 39*(4), 341–350.

Karababas, S., & Cather, H. (1994). Developing strategic information systems. *Integrated Manufacturing Systems, 5*(2), 4–11.

Khanagha, S., Volberda, H., & Oshri, I. (2014). Business model renewal and ambidexterity: Structural alteration and strategy formation process during transition to a Cloud business model. *R&D Management, 44*(3), 322–340.

Kolb, D. A. (1984). *Experiential learning: Experience as the source of learning and development.* Englewood Cliffs: Prentice Hall.

Kolb, D. A., Boyatzis, R. E., & Mainemelis, C. (2001). Experiential learning theory: Previous research and new directions. In *Perspectives on thinking learning and cognitive styles* (pp. 227–247). Mahwah: Lawrence Erlbaum Associates.

Langer, E. J. (1975). The illusion of control. *Journal of Personality and Social Psychology, 32*(2), 311–328.

Langer, E. J., & Roth, J. (1975). Heads I win, tails it's chance: The illusion of control as a function of the sequence of outcomes in a purely chance task. *Journal of Personality and Social Psychology, 32*(6), 951–955.

Levine, S., & White, P. E. (1961). Exchange as a conceptual framework for the study of interorganizational relationships. *Administrative Science Quarterly, 5*(4), 583–601.

Lewis, K., & Herndon, B. (2011). Transactive memory systems: Current issues and future research directions. *Organization Science, 22*(5), 1254–1265.

Lichtenstein, B. M. (1995). Evolution or transformation: A critique and alternative to punctuated equilibrium. In D. P. Moore (Ed.), *Academy of management best papers proceedings* (pp. 291–295). Madison: Omnipress.

Luehrman, T. A. (1998). Strategy as a portfolio of real options. *Harvard Business Review, 76*(5), 89–99.

Lyytinen, K. J. (1985). Implications of theories of language for information systems. *MIS Quarterly, 9*(1), 61–74.

Mandelbrot, B. B. (1983). *The fractal geometry of nature* (revised and enlarged ed.). New York: W.H. Freeman and Co.

March, J. G., & Simon, H. A. (1958). *Organizations. New York.* John Wiley & Sons, Ltd.

Markowitz, H. (1952). Portfolio selection. *The Journal of Finance, 7*(1), 77–91.

Martins, L. L., Rindova, V. P., & Greenbaum, B. E. (2015). Unlocking the hidden value of concepts: A cognitive approach to business model innovation. *Strategic Entrepreneurship Journal, 9*, 99–117.

McFarlan, W. F. (1981). Portfolio approach to information systems. *Harvard Business Review, 59*(5), 142–150.

Meyer, J. W., & Rowan, B. (1977). Institutionalized organizations: Formal structure as myth and ceremony. *American Journal of Sociology, 83*(2), 340–363.

Micheli, M. R., Berchicci, L., Ocasio, W., & Jansen, J. (2015). How managerial attention shapes business model innovation: Evidence from design industry. *Academy of management proceedings, 2015*(1), 13407. Academy of Management.

Miller, G. A. (1956). The magical number seven, plus or minus two: Some limits on our capacity for processing information. *Psychological Review, 63*(2), 81–97.

Miller, G. A., Galanter, E., & Pribram, K. H. (1960). *Plans and the structure of behavior.* New York: Rinehart & Winston.

Montgomery, H., Sharafi, P., & Hedman, L. R. (2004). Engaging in activities involving information technology: Dimensions, modes, and flow. *Human Factors: The Journal of the Human Factors and Ergonomics Society, 46*(2), 334–348.

Morgenstern, O., & Von Neumann, J. (1944). *Theory of games and economic behavior.* Princeton: Princeton University Press.

Myers, S. C. (1977). Determinants of corporate borrowing. *Journal of Financial Economics, 5*(2), 147–175.

Ocasio, W. (1997). Towards an attention based view of the firm. *Strategic Management Journal, 18*(S1), 187–206.

Ocasio, W. (2011). Attention to attention. *Organization Science, 22*(5), 1286–1296.

Peltokorpi, V. (2008). Transactive memory systems. *Review of General Psychology, 12*(4), 378–394.

Pettigrew, A. M. (1979). On studying organizational cultures. *Administrative Science Quarterly, 24*(4), 570–581.

Posen, H. E., Lee, J., & Yi, S. (2012). The power of imperfect imitation. *Strategic Management Journal, 34*(2), 149–164.

Premkumar, G., Ramamurthy, K., & Saunders, C. S. (2005). Information processing view of organizations: An exploratory examination of fit in the context of interorganizational relationships. *Journal of Management Information Systems, 22*(1), 257–294.

Presson, P. K., & Benassi, V. A. (1996). Illusion of control: A meta-analytic review. *Journal of Social Behavior and Personality, 11*(3), 493–510.

Qiu, L., & Benbasat, I. (2005). An investigation into the effects of Text-To-Speech voice and 3D avatars on the perception of presence and flow of live help in electronic commerce. *ACM Transactions on Computer-Human Interaction (TOCHI), 12*(4), 329–355.

Rahman, S. U. (1998). Theory of constraints: A review of the philosophy and its applications. *International Journal of Operations & Production Management, 18*(4), 336–355.

Ren, Y., & Argote, L. (2011). Transactive memory systems 1985–2010: An integrative framework of key dimensions, antecedents, and consequences. *The Academy of Management Annals, 5*(1), 189–229.

Rivkin, J. W. (2000). Imitation of complex strategies. *Management Science, 46*(6), 824–844.

Robertson, R., & Combs, A. (1995). *Chaos theory in psychology and the life sciences.* Hove: Psychology Press.

Romanelli, E., & Tushman, M. L. (1994). Organizational transformation as punctuated equilibrium: An empirical test. *Academy of Management Review, 37*(5), 1141–1166.

Sabatier, V., Kennard, A., & Mangematin, V. (2012). When technological discontinuities and disruptive business models challenge dominant industry logics : Insights from the drugs industry To cite this version : *Technological Forecasting and Social Change, 79*(5), 949–962.

Sarasvathy, S. (2001). Causation and effectuation: Toward a theoretical shift from inevitability to economic entrepreneurial contingency. *The Academy of Management Review, 26*(2), 243–263.

Sarasvathy, S. D. (2008). *Effectuation: Elements of entrepreneurial expertise.* Cheltenham: Edward Elgar Publishing.

Schein, E. H. (1985). *Organizational culture and leadership.* San Francisco: Jossey-Bass.

Schein, E. H. (1990). Organizational culture. *American Psychologist, 45*(2), 109–119.

Schein, E. H. (2010). *Organizational culture and leadership* (Vol. 2). New York: Wiley.

Schoop, M. (2001). An introduction to the language-action perspective. *ACM SIGGROUP Bulletin, 22*(2), 3–8.

Simon, H. A. (1947). *Administrative behavior; A study of decision-making processes in administrative organization.* New York: Macmillan.

Smircich, L. (1983). Concepts of culture and organizational analysis. *Administrative Science Quarterly, 28*(3), 339–358.

Stark, J. (2011). *Product lifecycle management.* London: Springer.

Teece, D. J. (2010). Business models, business strategy and innovation. *Long Range Planning, 43*(2–3), 172–194.

Thomke, S., & Manzi, J. (2014). The discipline of business experimentation. *Harvard Business Review, 92*(12), 70–79.

Thompson, J. M. T., & Stewart, H. B. (2002). *Nonlinear dynamics and chaos.* New York: Wiley.

Tikkanen, H., Lamberg, J.-A., Parvinen, P., & Kallunki, J.-P. (2005). Managerial cognition, action and the business model of the firm. *Management Decision, 43*(6), 789–809.

Toulmin, S. E. (1958). *The uses of argument.* Cambridge: Cambridge University Press.

Tushman, M. L., & Anderson, P. (1986). Technological discontinuities and organizational environments. *Administrative Science Quaterly, 31*(3), 439–465.

Tushman, M. L., & Romanelli, E. (1985). Organizational evolution: A metamorphisis model of convergence and reorientation. In L. L. Cummings & B. M. Staw (Eds.), *Research in organizational behavior* (Vol. 7, pp. 171–222). Greenwich: JAI Press.

Tversky, A., & Kahneman, D. (1981). The framing of decisions and the psychology of choice. *Science, 211*(4481), 453–458.

Van de Ven, A. H., & Poole, S. M. (1995). Explaining development and change in organizations. *Academy of Management Review, 20*, 510–540.

Walster, E., Berscheid, E., & Walster, G. W. (1973). New directions in equity research. *Journal of Personality and Social Psychology, 25*(2), 151–176.

Wegner, D. M. (1986). Transactive memory: A contemporary analysis of the group mind. In B. Mullen & G. R. Goethals (Eds.), *Theories of group behavior* (pp. 185–205). New York: Springer.

Whyte, G. (1986). Escalating commitment to a course of action: A reinterpretation. *Academy of Management Review, 11*(2), 311–321.

Wicklund, R. A., & Brehm, J. W. (1976). *Perspectives on cognitive dissonance.* New York: Halsted Press.

Winograd, T. (2006). Designing a new foundation for design. *Communications of the ACM, 49*(5), 71–74.

Winograd, T., & Flores, F. (1986). *Understanding computers and cognition: A new foundation for design.* Boston: Addison-Wesley Professional.

Winterhalter, S., Zeschky, M. B., & Gassmann, O. (2015). Managing dual business models in emerging markets: An ambidexterity perspective. *R&D Management, 46*, 464–479.

Wood, R., & Bandura, A. (1989). Social cognitive theory of organizational management. *The Academy of Management Review, 14*(3), 361–384.

Zellner, A. (1988). Optimal information processing and Bayes's theorem. *The American Statistician, 42*(4), 278–284.

Zollenkop, M. (2008). Changing business models and their impact on product development. In R. Schwientek, A. Schmidt, R. B. S. Consultants., & P. C. (Online S. Service) (Eds.), *Operations excellence smart solutions for business success* (pp. 9–23). New York: Palgrave Macmillan.

CHAPTER 5

Conclusion: Opening up a New Debate on BMI

Abstract This chapter summarizes the core contributions of the book, namely the organization of the business model field from a theoretical perspective and the explorative analysis of 50 theories. This included a study of both their application and their potential use for business model research. In doing so, more light into the principles and patterns of the black box BMI is shed. However, instead of providing answers right away, new questions for the field are presented. The conclusion points out how a new wave of business model research can be triggered. For instance, it suggests directing attention of research to the organizational dimension of business model innovation and the cognitive view on business models.

Keywords Business models • Business model innovation • Critical assessment of extant research • New perspectives • Outlook • Implications for business model research • Further management theories

Research on business models is on the rise, and we can confirm that this body of work is far more than just a subchapter of strategy, or a specific object in innovation research. In fact, it is becoming a new discipline in the more specialized field of management research. Ever since the first seminal works in the early 2000s, the topic has gained increasing attention in academia. However, as research is still in its infancy, much remains unanswered, especially from a theoretical stance. More than once, academia has highlighted that research should head for a broader theo-retical understanding of the concept. We enrich that ongoing debate and shed new light on it by following the unorthodox approach of exploring 50 theories in the context of business models and BMI.

The contribution of this research paper is threefold. First, it presents a broad literature review of the business model field and characterizes some of the most significant research groups. Second, it analyses 50 theories and a study of both their application and their potential for business model research. Consequently, third, the study yields several valuable insights for future research directions. It may even trigger a new wave of business model research coined by innovative theoretical anchoring.

In this regard, we point out that future attempts could focus on a theoretical foundation that drifts away from classic streams, such as the resource-based or knowledge-based views. Among the many potential future research directions, we would like to emphasize the promising organizational dimension in business model research. Only recently, research has taken up this challenge. Hence, we see several substreams emerging, for example, the successful management of dual or paral-lel business models (e.g. Casadesus-Masanell & Tarziján, 2012; Kim & Min, 2015; Velu & Stiles, 2013), antecedents of BMI (Amit & Zott, 2015; Frankenberger et al., 2014), and the business model as a unit of analysis in organizational ambidexterity (Winterhalter, Zeschky, & Gassmann, 2015). Since the implementation of BMIs requires a new holistic understanding that has not been covered sufficiently in the literature, this wave of publications is not surprising. Particularly underexplored theories in the organizational context of BMI are slack theory, transaction cost theory, and stakeholder theory.

Following the research group around Baden-Fuller, a further emerging theme in business model research is the cognitive view. This research argues that business models are cognitive devices through which managers organize their understanding about the logic of a firm (Martins, Rindova, & Greenbaum, 2015), and how managers make sense of their environment and drive strategic responses for it (Osiyevskyy & Dewald, 2015). In particular, the field of entrepreneur-ship applies this theoretical perspective to explain entrepreneurial cog-nition (Cacciotti & Hayton, 2015; Dew, Grichnik, Mayer-Haug, Read, & Brinckmann, 2015).

We attempted to compel a broad variety of theories and explored their application in business model research or vice versa. However, and

Table 5.1   Management theories on the phenomenon

General categories	Related theories	A new perspective on BMI
Org. theories	Contingency theory Organizational ambidexterity Garbage can theory General systems theory Language action perspective Management fashion theory New institutionalism Organizational culture theory Organizational information-processing theory Slack theory Stakeholder theory Transaction cost theory	*"BMI is an architectural alteration of a company's constituting managerial systems and structures"*
Cognitive theories	Attention-based view Managerial cognition Cognitive dissonance theory Social cognitive theory Effectuation Theory of illusion of control Self-efficacy theory	*"The business model is a mental construct that resides in the head of employees as schemas, initiating BMI is an intrinsic process"*
Rational/strategic choice theories	Game theory Portfolio theory Real options theory	*"BMI is a stream of decisions"*
Resource-based theories	Theory of constraints Theory of dynamic capabilities Resource-based view of the firm Resource dependency theory	*"BMI is the renewal of a firm's unique competitive resource base and advantages"*
Knowledge and learning-based theories	Absorptive capacity theory Experiential learning theory Information processing theory Knowledge-based view of the firm Organizational learning theory Transactive memory theory	*"BMI is a process of continuous knowledge conversion that requires absorptive capacities"*
Evolutionary theories	Chaos theory Competitive imitation Evolutionism Historical institutionalism Product lifecycle model Punctuated equilibrium theory	*"BMI is a continuous process of experimentation and adaptation of the status-quo to the changing external environment"*

(continued)

Table 5.1   (continued)

General categories	Related theories	A new perspective on BMI
Behavioural theories	Administrative behaviour theory Agency theory Theory of argumentation Behavioural decision theory Equity theory Institutional theory Flow theory Prospect theory Yield shift theory of satisfaction	*"BMI is triggered by the employees' behaviour, developing the firm towards a status of equilibrium"*
Social theories	Social capital theory Social exchange theory Social network theory Structuration theory	*"BMI is enabled by a network of social interactions in which persons are acting in bounded rationality"*

inherent to this approach, there are several shortcomings. In order to draw a holistic picture, many additional theories should be considered, such as the theory of reasoned action, the theory of planned behaviour, the upper echelons theory, or self-determination theory. Although there is no claim for completeness in this study, it nonetheless provides a broad review and basis to trigger novel thoughts and debates.

In summary, an overview of the analysed theories structured in eight overarching categories is given (i.e. organizational, cognitive, rational/strategic choice, resource-based, knowledge/learning-based, evolutionary, behavioural, and social constructivist theories). Table 5.1 depicts how each of the theoretical viewpoints could consider the phenomena of the *business model* and *BMI* in a new manner. There are many promising future pathways for innovative business model and BMI research, which can and should be guided within a fitting, yet appealing theoretical framework.

BIBLIOGRAPHY

Amit, R., & Zott, C. (2015). Crafting business architecture: The antecedents of business model design. *Strategic Entrepreneurship Journal, 9*(4), 331–350.

Cacciotti, G., & Hayton, J. C. (2015). Fear and entrepreneurship: A review and research agenda. *International Journal of Management Reviews, 17*(2), 165–190.

Casadesus-Masanell, R., & Tarziján, J. (2012, February). When one business model isn't enough. *Harvard Business Review, 90*, 132–137.

Dew, N., Grichnik, D., Mayer-Haug, K., Read, S., & Brinckmann, J. (2015). Situated entrepreneurial cognition. *International Journal of Management Reviews, 17*(2), 143–164.

Frankenberger, K., Weiblen, T., & Gassmann, O. (2014). The antecedents of open business models: An exploratory study of incumbent firms. *R&D Management, 44*(2), 173–188.

Kim, S. K., & Min, S. (2015). Business model innovation performance: When does adding a new business model benefit an incumbent? *Strategic Entrepreneurship Journal, 9*, 34–57.

Martins, L. L., Rindova, V. P., & Greenbaum, B. E. (2015). Unlocking the hidden value of concepts: A cognitive approach to business model innovation. *Strategic Entrepreneurship Journal, 9*, 99–117.

Osiyevskyy, O., & Dewald, J. (2015). Explorative versus exploitative business model change: The cognitive antecedents of firm-level responses to disruptive innovation. *Strategic Entrepreneurship Journal, 9*(1), 58–78.

Velu, C., & Stiles, P. (2013). Managing decision-making and cannibalization for parallel business models. *Long Range Planning, 46*(6), 443–458.

Winterhalter, S., Zeschky, M. B., & Gassmann, O. (2015). Managing dual business models in emerging markets: An ambidexterity perspective. *R&D Management, 46*, 464–479.

INDEX[1]

[1] Note: Page number followed by 'n' refers to endnotes.

© The Editor(s) (if applicable) and the Author(s) 2016

O. Gassmann et al., *Exploring the Field of Business Model Innovation*,

DOI 10.1007/978-3-319-41144-6

113

Printed in the United States
By Bookmasters